insight text guide

Ross Walker

Romulus, My Father

Raimond Gaita

First published in 2004, reprinted in 2006, 2007, 2008, 2015, 2019.

Insight Publications Pty Ltd
3/350 Charman Road
Cheltenham VIC 3192
Australia
Tel: +61 3 8571 4950
Fax: +61 3 8571 0257
Email: books@insightpublications.com.au

www.insightpublications.com.au

National Library of Australia Cataloguing-in-Publication entry:
Walker, Ross, 1957- .
Romulus my father, Raimond Gaita.
For senior secondary English students.
ISBN 9781920693626 (paperback).
1. Gaita, Raimond, 1946- —Criticism and interpretation.
2. Gaita, Raimond, 1946- Romulus, my father. I. Title.
(Series : Insight text guide).
304.8940497092

Cover design: The Modern Art Production Group

Printed in Australia

contents

CHARACTER MAP

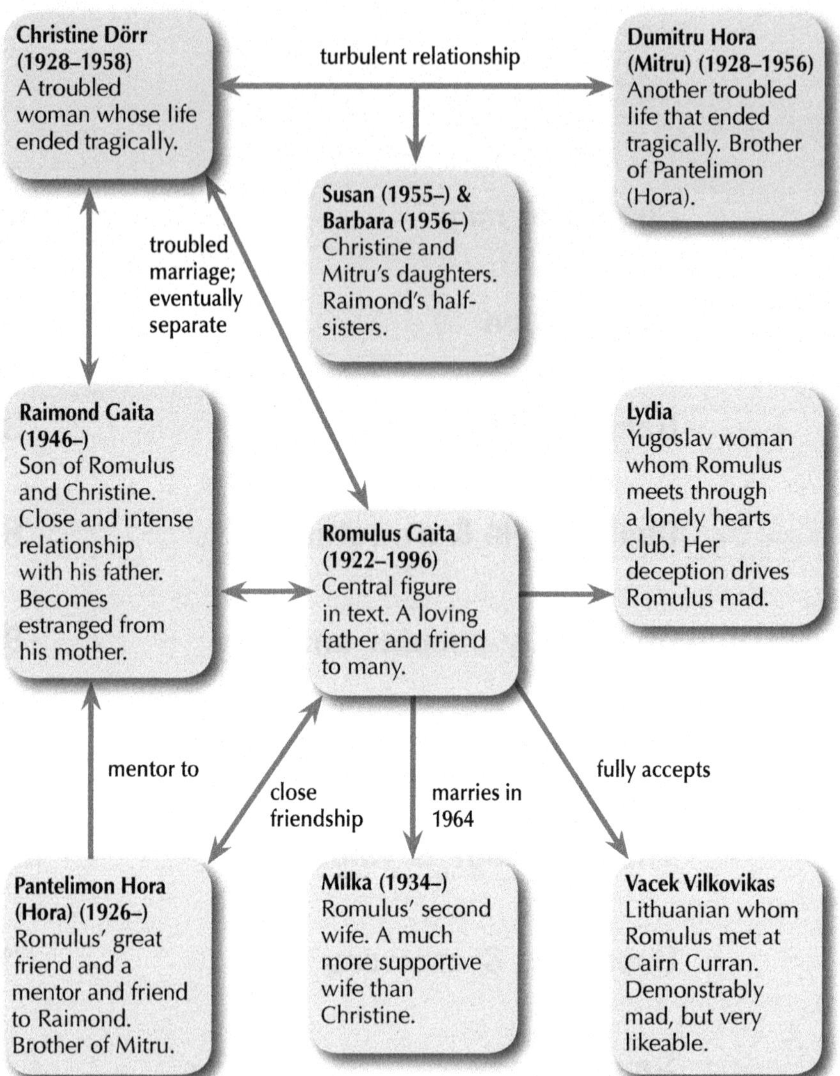

INTRODUCTION

Relationships between parents and children are fundamental both to our lives and to almost all writing that attempts to comprehend the meaning of human experiences. Some of the most compelling drama of life takes place inside the family home, and *Romulus, My Father* has such drama in abundance. In Raimond Gaita's hands, a biography about 'a good and unusual man' (p.163) becomes a good and unusual biography. The book opens for us a window onto the period and place in which Romulus and his family lived. It is not surprising that *Romulus, My Father* won the Victorian Premier's Literary Award of 1998, for it is not just an elegantly written biography of an interesting man. The author's personal background as a moral philosopher gives his memoir an added dimension; it addresses fundamental human issues, giving it a wider importance. Raimond Gaita touches on vital questions: are people ennobled by suffering? Is it better to suffer an injury than to cause one? And perhaps the most important question: what is a good life? What does it mean to be a good person, to live well?

For Romulus, this question was central. Nothing mattered as much for him as to live decently; his whole identity was shaped by this strong moral concern. This made Romulus an unusual man indeed, for it is rare to find people who hold so unswervingly to their core values. It is rare, too, to find people who think so conscientiously about their life and how to live it. We can be thankful that Raimond Gaita's remarkable skills as a writer have brought to us a story that might easily have never been told.

The book has an inspirational quality. One critic has remarked:

> *Romulus, My Father* is about the kind of man [Romulus] was, and his responses to the pressures that came upon him. That straight away gives this book a lasting value beyond that of a mere narrative; it gives it the value of a model for life and conduct in trying circumstances. We see that partly through

> his behaviour towards his son, and especially in the values and attitudes he impressed on his son, for which Raimond is constantly grateful.[1]

Gaita's memoir is of interest, too, as a social history of life in rural Victoria from the 1940s to 1960s. While this period would still remain relatively fresh in the memories of older readers, for most students of this text in the early years of the twenty-first century this period might well seem quite foreign. Australians now, by and large, take for granted the multicultural society in which we live. In the early years of Raimond Gaita's life, though, Australian society was still largely monocultural. When Romulus Gaita came to this country in 1946, Australia for the first time was being opened up to large-scale immigration from Europe. The turbulent aftermath of World War II provided the trigger for this movement.

About Raimond Gaita

Raimond Gaita describes himself as 'a citizen who happens to be a philosopher'. Although he asserts that 'the influence of philosophy in public affairs has been a disaster',[2] philosophy is his natural bent and strongly shapes his thinking. From role models such as his father and Hora, his father's closest friend, he has acquired a deep intellectual curiosity. Gaita shares another of his father's characteristics – a generosity of spirit, a reluctance to judge other people harshly. He has described his father as 'morally intense, but not at all judgemental'[3] and he displays those qualities himself.

---

1 Richard Johnson, 'Romulus, My Father – Raimond Gaita', Council of Adult Education Website, http://www.cae.edu.au/bookgroups/radionat.html (note that this page is no longer available).

2 Raimond Gaita, talk at Writers' Festival, Melbourne, 28 February 2004.

3 Gaita, talk at Writers' Festival.

BACKGROUND & CONTEXT

Yugoslavia – Romulus' country of birth

Although Romulus Gaita always thought of himself as Romanian, it was in the Eastern European country of Yugoslavia that he was born. This country has endured a long history of violence and strife. The ethnic and religious rivalries that have plagued it continue today. The three main ethnic groups that comprise the Yugoslavian population – the Serbs, the Croats and the Slovenes – hold conflicting political and ethnic traditions that have sown the seeds of disunity. Not even invasion by the Axis forces (Germany and Italy) during World War II (1939–45) motivated these rival groups to settle their differences. During this war, 1,700,000 Yugoslavs were killed, about one million of them by other Yugoslavs.

During this war, the European Axis forces invaded Yugoslavia. Germany set up a puppet 'Independent State of Croatia' and unleashed a reign of terror. As the war turned against the Axis, Josef Broz Tito, the leader of the Partisans, the largest of the Yugoslav resistance groups, travelled secretly to Moscow and arranged for the Soviets (Russians) to enter Yugoslavia. Tito became Prime Minister in March 1945, setting up a Soviet-style constitution. Between 1945 and 1948 Tito punished wartime collaborators, frequently by execution. Many Yugoslavs left the country because of their distaste for the new Communist regime; among them was Romulus' great friend Hora, whose antipathy towards Communism is made plain in the course of the book. And many left in a search for a more peaceful and prosperous country. Those who found their way to Australia would have seen it as a country free from the upheavals they had experienced – among them was Romulus Gaita.

World War II and its aftermath

The period between 1939 – when war broke out and Romulus, now in Germany, was conscripted into an army of foreign workers to serve the German war effort – and 1950, when he came to Australia with his wife and son, must have been most difficult. The racist policies of Adolf Hitler's Nazi regime targeted people of Slavic descent, such as Romulus. Nazi ideology regarded such people as racially inferior, suitable only for factory work if indeed even for that. Furthermore, the city of Dortmund, to which Romulus was sent, was constantly under aerial bombardment from Allied forces. After the destruction of Hitler's regime, life continued to be harsh. Germany was left devastated, and shortages of food and other basic necessities would have been the rule.

Migrant experiences in Australia

The immigrant story is central to Australian history. In the years following the upheaval of World War II, successive Australian governments encouraged European migration to Australia. At the end of the war, our population was only about seven million – very small for such a large country. Yet not all immigrants were welcomed without reservation. *Romulus, My Father* shows us some of the challenges confronted by such people in moving from the Old World to the New World. Many skilled migrants had the frustration of being unable to find employment befitting their special skills; this was Romulus' experience.

We see, too, how Romulus was faced in Australia with a culture very different from that to which he had been accustomed. We can speculate about how strange and foreign life in a small country town such as Maryborough would have been for Europeans like Romulus and Christine. The countryside there is flat and dry, and at the time cultural life would have been limited. Supremely adaptable, Romulus was able to live and work successfully in the area, but his wife, Christine, clearly found it impossible to adapt.

In 1950, when Romulus and his small family came to Australia, this country was still emerging from the hardships of war. Life in rural Victoria in the 1940s and 1950s would have been vastly less affluent for most people than it is today. Clearly, Romulus' life was not easy, though undeniably easier than it would have been in Yugoslavia and post-war Germany, where he lived before coming to Australia. For the 'baby boomers' (a name given to those born in the years immediately following the war) such as Raimond Gaita, Australia was to become a country enjoying a prosperity which their parents could hardly have imagined. The years following Raimond's birth in 1946 were years of changing values and opportunities. Gaita's memoir paints a picture of some of those changes, thus providing a social history of one part of Australia at that time.

GENRE, STYLE & STRUCTURE

Genre

While *Romulus, My Father* could well be classified as a biography or a personal memoir, this classification may be too simplistic. We need to remember that biography is always dependent on the memory of the writer – and memories tend to alter due to the passage of time, or the emotional loading attached to them. It has been said that anything processed by memory is fiction. While this claim may be going a little too far, it is a useful notion, recognising as it does the inevitable overlap between fiction and nonfiction. We are not reading a police court record of events when we read a personal memoir, precisely because it is just that – personal, and therefore subjective. 'The facts of the past are unchangeable', writes Gaita, 'but meaning is seldom fixed'.[4]

Keeping in mind all these things, I think we can conclude that Raimond Gaita is blessed with a remarkable memory, and this gives us confidence in the veracity of his memoir. The detail with which he relates so many of the events in the book is very convincing. He is an observant and perceptive witness, often able to describe how he felt while a particular event was unfolding, where exactly he was, what people were wearing, and the like.

Gaita tells us that some of the material in his book was distilled into the eulogy he gave at his father's funeral. We can thus view his work as a personal tribute to Romulus. The title of the work is significant, showing as it does the author's sense of pride at being the son of this man. For other works of personal tribute, you might be interested to read Brian Matthews' memoir *A Fine and Private Place*, which focuses on the author's early life in St Kilda, or Susan Cheever's *Home Before Dark*, a moving memoir of her father, the American novelist and short story writer John Cheever.

---

4 Raimond Gaita, *The Philosopher's Dog*, Text Publishing, Melbourne, 2002, p.97.

But *Romulus, My Father* is not only a biography of Romulus. As the narrator, Raimond Gaita is inevitably a central figure in his own story. We can read the book as an autobiographical memoir detailing his own early life. Although Gaita keeps his own reactions in the background, reserving centre stage for his father, his narrative at almost every point shows how his father's life directly shaped and influenced his own.

The memoir as a novel

There are anecdotes in *Romulus, My Father* that remind us of the old adage, 'truth is stranger than fiction'. For example, you were probably astonished, as I was, by the story of the moment when Romulus matter-of-factly announced to his son that they had to go immediately to Melbourne so that he could shoot Lydia's husband. Then there is the episode describing how the family friend 'M' came to Lydia's mother's bed and she received him happily, thinking all the while that she was sleeping with Romulus. One reviewer, Jamie Grant, commented that the book is 'as compelling to read as a novel',[5] and there certainly are passages when we feel as if we are in fact reading a novel. Gaita himself alerts us in his Author's note that 'to protect their identities' he has 'changed the names of several of the people in this book', in much the same way that a novelist would when using real-life experience as the raw material for their story.

Style

We do not have to read much of this book to see that it is excellently written. It is studded with sentences that are striking because of the cleanness and elegance with which they are formulated. The author knows what to include and what to omit, and how to highlight the essentials. The style is very lucid, often matter of fact. Some of Gaita's stories are lurid, but he tells them in a low-key way which adds to their impact. His style never draws attention to itself. He allows the circumstances he describes

5 Quoted in the front pages of the text.

to speak for themselves, without intrusive authorial comment. Another virtue of the book is the author's humour and sense of the ridiculous – again, presented in a very dry, low-key manner.

Structure

By and large, Gaita tells his story in chronological order, starting at the beginning and working through to the end of Romulus' life. He starts with Romulus' early life in Yugoslavia, and progresses through to his years in Germany, the many years in Victoria, the high and low points of his life, and his short final illness and death. An interesting feature of the book's structure is the way Gaita alternates between stories of his father's and his mother's lives. But it's important to remember that this isn't just a biography of Romulus and his family, but a narrative that includes other people as well. Between the life stories of Romulus, Raimond and Christine, Gaita interweaves the stories of many other people, giving his work wider human interest.

Q To what extent are our identities shaped by what we remember?

CHAPTER-BY-CHAPTER ANALYSIS

Chapter 1 (pp.1–10)

Summary: *Romulus' childhood in Yugoslavia; he goes to Germany; he is conscripted into an army of foreign workers there; Romulus and Christine meet; their courtship and marriage; the birth of Raimond; the family emigrates to Australia.*

The opening plunges us into a world that would be strange and unfamiliar to most readers. The narrative begins with an arresting image of danger and potential violence: the thirteen-year-old Romulus wards off his chronically drunken uncle with a pitchfork. Gaita clearly begins this way to emphasise the harshness of his father's early life. It is an image of childhood destroyed, a theme that we will see unfold in Raimond's early life. 'Childhood as we now know it, a space apart from the adult world, a life of its own', we are told, 'did not exist in that part of the world at that time' (p.2). The simple, declarative sentence 'He was thirteen years old' (p.2), coming at the end of two paragraphs detailing the extraordinary difficulties of Romulus' life, is meant to shock us with the reality of what a boy of such tender years had to endure.

Romulus was almost totally thrown back on his own resources: he set out across Yugoslavia to find work, presumably on his own; he had to contribute to the family's finances; he had to threaten his uncle with a pitchfork to protect himself. The circumstances of his life were dire, but there is no doubt that they helped build the remarkable resourcefulness and self-reliance which characterised Romulus' adult life. We see that the proverb 'the child is father to the man' is true for him. This period of his life must have helped Romulus form his view that life is hard and that struggle is an inevitable condition of it.

We learn of other qualities that Romulus would display through the whole of his life. As a boy he learned easily, already showing the considerable intellectual curiosity of his adult life, an asset that he clearly passed on to his son. Not even the threat of beatings could stop him from reading surreptitiously under his desk at school. He displayed, too, the 'deeply religious spirit' (p.3) that nourished the rest of his life. His early fondness for Bible stories no doubt helped to develop his lifelong love of stories; telling stories became for him, as for many people, a way of making sense of life.

It is saddening (and maddening) to learn that Romulus' chance of entering secondary school was dashed merely because of the shortcomings of 'an inefficient postal service' (p.3). Both as a boy and as a man, he was a person for whom the circumstances of life were often those of defeat and deprivation. We cannot help but feel for him, as he somehow embodies all those people who have deserved far better lives than they had.

There is something inspiring about the way Romulus dealt with hardship. He seems never to have complained about his lot. He was 'a man of practical genius' (p.4), using his skills in making or repairing to earn the money that was denied him during his apprenticeship as a blacksmith. His ability 'to make almost anything to the most exacting standards', to do work that was 'unsurpassed in quality' (p.5), was a reflection of the high standards which he applied in every area of his life.

Q To what extent do you think Romulus would have been damaged by his early life?

Q Did he benefit from his early hardships in any way?

Romulus meets Christine

Another stage of Romulus' life began when he went to Germany with a view to practising his trade in more favourable circumstances and, on the outbreak of war, was conscripted into an army of foreign workers to serve the war effort. It was in Dortmund that he met and fell in love with Christine Anna Dörr, Raimond's mother. Their relationship was dangerous not only because Romulus' Slavic origins would have made both of them 'victims of Nazi racial policy' (p.7), but because of the highly emotional temperaments of each. It isn't surprising that the union of two people, each so volatile, should come to grief. She was 'prone to tempestuous jealousy' (p.8); he tried to shoot himself when she left him early in their relationship. We see here Romulus' emotional instability, which blighted his life and which formed such a striking contrast to his wonderful reliability.

We see, too, the first signs of Christine's emotional illness. Clearly she was psychologically and emotionally unequipped for motherhood; as Gaita states bluntly, 'she seemed incapable of taking care of me' (p.8). The story that Raimond's grandmother told before giving birth to Christine – 'she dreamed of Jesus who appeared to her bloody and showing the wounds of the crucifixion' (p.8) – seemed, so the grandmother concluded, to foreshadow the suffering that Christine would endure. Or perhaps the story actually contributed to that suffering. Christine's mother's distress at experiencing the dream, and Christine's distress at hearing of it, may well have made the prediction a self-fulfilling prophecy. Whatever the truth, the image of crucifixion was a particularly apt symbol of what Christine's life was to become for her and for those around her.

Gaita relates a second prophecy at the end of this chapter. A fortune teller predicted, before Romulus' passage to Australia with his wife and son, that 'he would lose his wife and suffer greatly' (p.10). Whether or not we attach credibility to clairvoyants, in the light of what we have learned about Romulus and Christine the prophecy is worrying; the chapter ends on an ominous note.

Q Romulus later told Christine that 'he did not marry her because he loved her' (p.8). What do you think led Romulus and Christine to marry?

Chapter 2 (pp.11–19)

Summary: *The family arrives in Australia; life at Bonegilla; Romulus is sent to Baringhup, splitting up the family; the Hora brothers (Pantelimon and Mitru) enter the story; Christine is unfaithful; the move to Frogmore.*

At first, Raimond and his mother remained at the migrant reception and clearing camp in north-eastern Victoria, while Romulus was sent to the central Victorian town of Baringhup to work on the Cairn Curran reservoir project. (Public works such as this reservoir provided employment for new migrants in the 1940s and 1950s; the Snowy River Hydro-Electric project in New South Wales was another example.)

In the camp at Baringhup Romulus met the two Romanian brothers, Pantelimon (known as Hora) and Dumitru (Mitru), with whom he quickly made friends. They were refugees from the oppressive communist regime in Romania. Both were well educated and striking in appearance, but Hora was of stronger character – as we see clearly in the rest of the narrative.

Difficulties in the new country

We learn in this chapter of the prejudice directed against 'New Australians' such as Romulus. Despite his remarkable practical skills, he was given menial manual work only, as were many skilled migrants. His uncomplaining attitude to this injustice is fatalistic: he 'had long come to accept what fate dealt him' (p.16).

It was obviously harder for Romulus to adapt himself to the landscape of central Victoria; 'even after more than forty years' he could not reconcile himself to it (p.14). The typically Australian eucalypts to him (as also to Christine) 'seemed symbols of deprivation and barrenness' (p.14). No doubt this landscape, so starkly different from that of Europe, reminded him of how far he was from the land of his birth. He never came to love the Australian countryside as Raimond did – Raimond's perspective would of course have been unaffected by memories of Europe. We are reminded that beauty is indeed in the eye of the beholder, and how that eye sees is shaped by previous experience. To Raimond Gaita 'the landscape is one of rare beauty', but 'to a European or English eye it seems desolate' (p.14).

Family troubles

Gaita describes the signs of his mother's instability of character, which manifested in her extramarital relationships and her obvious neglect of Raimond, so serious that he had to move to Baringhup to be cared for by his father. The tension that news of her behaviour caused for Romulus began to emerge. We learn of his fierce temper, which exploded when he smacked Raimond very hard for lying about the theft of a bottle of aftershave lotion. A small infraction by a child grew into an episode of domestic disaster as a result of this overreaction. The main cause of Romulus' rage was the fact that he suspected his son of lying; for the first time we see the high value Romulus placed on truthfulness. Clearly, this incident from Raimond's early life has remained in his memory because it was so powerful emotionally.

Q Do some research on the contribution that migrants made to the Snowy River Hydro-Electric project in New South Wales.

Q Find out about the Bonegilla camp in north-eastern Victoria.

Chapter 3 (pp.21–34)

Summary: *Life at Frogmore; Romulus finds work at a tool factory in Maryborough; Christine moves to Melbourne with Mitru; her emotional problems grow worse.*

This chapter begins with a striking description of the small farmhouse called Frogmore where the family took up residence. Gaita paints a picture of a house, and a family, at the mercy of the elements: a storm blew the washhouse clean away; rats invaded the house; there were few trees to soften the prevailing harshness. Trees, in fact, became symbols of aspects of life in this place. The peppercorns 'were planted as though to mediate between local and European landscapes' (p.23), as if they, like the European migrants in this area, were caught between two worlds. And the dead red gum near the house became for Christine 'a symbol of her desolation' (p.23).

Christine and Mitru

Christine appears quite out of place in this landscape. As a 'troubled city girl from Central Europe', she could not adapt to life 'in a dilapidated farmhouse in a landscape that highlighted her isolation' (pp.24–5). We can surmise that her feelings of loneliness and insecurity would have heightened her tendency towards promiscuity. It was at this stage that she began her sexual relationship with Mitru, a man of whom Raimond became very fond. His compassion for this troubled man is evident in everything he writes about him. Mitru had many admirable qualities, but he suffered from a 'pain' the severity of which few others could understand. His relationship with Christine was problematic, involving as it did adultery and frequent infidelities. He felt distress over her unfaithfulness and her neglect of Raimond, and probably he also felt a sense of guilt that the relationship involved adultery.

Raimond's unsettled childhood

Life for Raimond must have been difficult, whether living with his mother in St Kilda or with his father at Frogmore. He tells of what could have been the beginning of a career in juvenile delinquency, describing the 'petty thieving and begging' that he and a friend practised around the streets of St Kilda (p.26). Such behaviour could well have stemmed from a feeling of deprivation engendered by his mother's neglect of him. His mother's attitude can be seen from Raimond's observation that after the police had left the house, she smacked him, 'more because she was humiliated than because she was seriously troubled by what I had done' (p.27).

For a small child, long nights alone such as Raimond spent at Frogmore must have been frightening. His description of the area surrounding the house at night – it sounds like the setting for a horror movie – re-creates a sense of fear that he has obviously never forgotten. Perhaps the only positive to emerge from these circumstances was that they fostered Raimond's growing love of animals. It must have been a great comfort to him to have the dogs sleeping in his bed during those lonely nights.

Two anecdotes about Romulus

While Romulus is not at the centre of this chapter, two anecdotes relating to him are noteworthy. One is the amusing story of the fire he accidentally started while trying to kill a snake (p.28). The word 'overkill' is appropriate to describe this. The other is the story of how Romulus, with his quick thinking, helped to save Neil Mikkelsen's life after he fell off a ladder while building a haystack (pp.28–9). This action epitomised Romulus' basic goodness as a human being, and it is appropriate that Gaita should mention it again at the end of the book, when he describes Mikkelsen's continuing gratitude to his father.

Christine's depression

The last section of the chapter (pp.30–4) is very dark. It describes the extent to which Christine's depression overpowered her. Her habit of sitting, just staring into the fire, is typical of the behaviour of a person depressed almost to the point of catatonia (a condition in which the sufferer falls into a stupor, often alternating with phases of excitement). And yet, Gaita recalls that 'at the time she appeared ... cheerful and vivacious, even when she lay in bed during the day' (pp.30–1). She was complex and troubled, a person with strong instincts towards both life and death. Gaita describes his mother as having 'the arresting presence of someone who experienced the world with a thoughtful intensity' (p.31) – and Romulus was clearly similar in this. Perhaps this shared quality helped initially to draw them together.

Christine emerges here as a tragic figure who certainly merits our sympathy. She was 'desperately lonely' (p.31); this must have worsened her depression. In the 1950s there was far less understanding of depression than there is today; mental illness was stigmatised and the treatments available were much more limited. And it must have been very difficult to find adequate medical and psychological support in a small country town, as is made plain when we learn that a mere two days after her suicide attempt Christine was sent back to Frogmore, presumably with no promise of continuing treatment.

Raimond himself witnessed the immediate effects of Christine's suicide attempt, which would have been deeply traumatising for a small child. It would also have been distressing for Raimond to see his mother in the state she was in after she returned home from the hospital in Maldon. We naturally feel for her, too, as she is remembered here: a frail, ill woman who 'appeared forsaken', swamped by a vast, indifferent landscape (p.32). This woman was dying while still alive – she looked 'as though she had returned from the dead, unsure about the value of the achievement', as Gaita neatly puts it (p.32).

Other distressing incidents are related towards the end of this chapter. On one occasion, Christine wandered away at night, causing the police to search a nearby swamp, and she returned cut and bleeding the following morning. Imagine the anxiety that Romulus and Raimond must have felt, having to endure episodes of such erratic behaviour. Gaita relates the incident with an unembellished directness that emphasises its horror. Especially poignant is the information that Christine had injured herself falling over a log and had spent the night sleeping beside it. No other image could depict so clearly her painful loneliness, helplessness and isolation.

The last sentence of the chapter informs us that, after Christine returned to Melbourne to live with Mitru, her marriage to Romulus was effectively finished. When Romulus wrote to Christine he now addressed her as 'Dear Madam', as if addressing a stranger, and signed himself 'R. Gaita' (p.34). It seems incongruous that he could address the mother of his child this way; his sense of hurt must have gone very deep.

Q To what extent did Raimond suffer from the lack of a stable mother?

Chapter 4 (pp.35–56)

Summary: *Romulus' animals and their importance; Romulus starts a poultry farm; his motorcycle accident; Hora steps in to look after Raimond; the incident of the razor.*

Romulus and his animals

The chapter opens by introducing a theme that becomes significant in the rest of the narrative: the importance of animals in the lives of Romulus and Raimond, and the comfort and company that animals bring to humans. It has been said that we can measure a person's humanity by the way they treat animals, and Romulus' very humane treatment of them reflected the deep respect that he granted to all sentient beings. Of the four animals mentioned here – 'Rusha the cow, Marta the cat, Orloff the dog and … Jack the cockatoo' (p.35) – Jack was clearly the most remarkable, so much so that he becomes a character in his own right. He was intensely loyal to Romulus and loved him deeply, as we can see from his habit of coming into Romulus' bed, putting his beak to his lips as if to kiss him, and saying 'Tsk tsk tsk, tsk tsk tsk' which Raimond assumed meant 'I love you' (p.38). You can read more about Orloff the dog in Gaita's later work, *The Philosopher's Dog*. His story is told very briefly in this chapter, a story of a wonderful animal who met a very cruel death.

Romulus has an accident – and Hora comes to the rescue

In this chapter we learn of the first of Romulus' serious motorcycle accidents. We can't help but feel that his emotional nature, coupled with the stresses under which he lived, contributed to his proneness to accidents. On this occasion, it was quarrelling with Mitru and Christine prior to riding that was to blame (pp.42–3). An important consequence of this accident was the arrival at Frogmore of Hora, who left his job in North Melbourne in order to take care of Raimond while Romulus was recuperating in hospital.

Thus developed one of the most important relationships of Raimond's life. Hora was a man of great kindness; he took extraordinary trouble to look after Raimond. It is evident that he saw Christine as a threat to Raimond's future security and in his role *in loco parentis* (in the place of a parent) he insisted that she leave.

The razor

Some time after Romulus' return from hospital the incident in which Raimond took a cut-throat razor belonging to his father occurred. This incident brings to our minds the earlier one about the aftershave, as it again shows Romulus' uncompromising insistence on honesty and truthfulness. This was one of the most marked features of his personality. Why, then, wouldn't Raimond trust his father when Romulus told him that he would escape punishment if he simply told the truth?

We begin to learn in this chapter of the range of responsibilities that Raimond was expected to shoulder – far more than most boys of such a young age. He had to take over many of the tasks that would have been his mother's, such as cooking and cleaning. Nevertheless, we sense that in this period a more stable home environment was emerging – there seems to have been a welcomely predictable domestic rhythm developing. We read that Romulus had the opportunity to harness his talents as a blacksmith; he was a creative, productive man, a great worker happy in his work. This seems like a classic case of a one-parent family working more happily than a two-parent one in which one of the parents is dysfunctional.

The chapter ends on a happier note than the previous one, with the introduction into the narrative of the two sisters, Miss Collard and Mrs Lillie, and a delightful anecdote about Miss Collard's irreverent humour.

Q Consider the incident of the razor. Why do you think Raimond didn't trust his father enough to tell him the truth?

Q Look at some of Raimond Gaita's anecdotes in the book. Why do you think they have been included? Why do you think they have remained in Gaita's memory?

Chapter 5 (pp.57–74)

Summary: *Raimond's essay about Elvis Presley; Raimond's epiphany; Vacek introduced; swimming in the dam; Raimond's bond with Hora grows, as does his love of reading and his interest in the life of the mind.*

Raimond's essay about Elvis Presley

Raimond's lack of a mother in his life worried Romulus as well as Mrs Lillie and Miss Collard, and other women in the area. Romulus' concern was heightened by an incident that occurred when Raimond was eleven – so this would have been in 1957. The incident related to Raimond's growing fascination with Elvis Presley, who was then in his heyday as one of the world's most popular entertainers. He was also a symbol of conflict between the younger and older generations. Some people feared that Presley's uninhibited and overtly sexual body language – he was known as 'Elvis the Pelvis' because of the way he gyrated that part of his body – would corrupt the youth of the day.

Presley's song 'Baby Let's Play House' is a fairly steamy song with obvious sexual overtones, so it is not surprising that it had a powerful effect on a boy then on the cusp of adolescence. And no doubt the fact that the girl in whose company he heard the song was a fan of Presley further encouraged Raimond's interest in the singer. Raimond's creation of a book about Presley, including Raimond's own 'passionate text praising rock and roll' (p.59), was unusual for a boy of that age – or of any age. It was an early sign of that impulse towards self-expression that drives most writers, and also a declaration of independence from his father and the values embodied by his generation.

We may ask the question: why did Raimond leave the book on the kitchen table, where his father was bound to see it? I think it is too simplistic to say that he did this just to provoke his father by setting himself up in opposition to him. The budding writer inside Raimond was beginning to stir, and he was no doubt proud of what he had created and wanted to show it off. He was, at this stage of his life, beginning to emerge as a deeply thoughtful and cerebral person, very different from other 'farm boys'.

Raimond's epiphany

This observation segues into the next major episode recounted in this chapter, the story of Raimond's epiphany – a moment of sudden and powerful revelation – when he went out into the bush intending to shoot a rabbit. This was a defining moment of his life, about which he also writes in *The Philosopher's Dog*. It was the moment when his feeling about the countryside changed, as the surrounding trees were wondrously transfigured by the quality of the light 'which so sharply delineated them against a dark blue sky' (p.61). Describing the experience in distinctly religious terms, he continues: 'It was as though God had taken me to the back of his workshop and shown me something really special' (p.61). Raimond's deep responsiveness to the world around him was beginning to grow into a strong sense of its sacredness. To kill a rabbit now would have been to him a violation of that response. He felt at one with the world and everything in it.

Q Write about a moment that changed your view of life (or of some aspect of it; or write a story embodying such a moment).

Q Compare Raimond's response to the countryside with his father's.

Q Do some research about Elvis Presley and his influence on popular culture.

Raimond's love of reading – and an inspiring teacher

Gaita notes that 'this encounter with a transcendent natural beauty drove [him] deeper into the world of books' (p.62). His embracing of the world of ideas was encouraged not only by his father, but also by Ronald Mottek, the local primary school teacher. That this man was of foreign origin and unconventional by nature would likely have added to his appeal. He brought knowledge of the wider world to his small country town. He seems to have been an inspirational teacher, and his influence extended beyond the classroom. His personal concern for both Raimond and Romulus is evident from his advice to Raimond: 'Be careful what you do. If you were to do anything bad, if you were to be in trouble with the police, the disappointment would kill your father' (p.63). Just how much Romulus cared for Raimond was underscored by his overheard remark to Mrs Smolak: 'My son is everything to me' (p.64).

Vacek

At this stage, we are introduced to Vacek Vilkovikas, the eccentric, indeed mad, Lithuanian. He is like a character from a novel, and this is one of the parts of the book that reads rather like fiction. Vacek lived between two boulders; he cooked food in his own urine; and he used to come to the window of the Gaitas' house looking like a figure from a horror film. Yet for all that, he had attractive qualities: he was intelligent, gentle – despite his frightening appearance – and he had an admirable 'sense of communion with animals' (p.67). The anecdotes about Orloff and the sausages, and about the grub that fell onto the car Vacek was washing, are very touching.

Hora

The rest of this chapter focuses on Raimond's growing relationship with Hora, Romulus' great friend. We are given attractive descriptions of the swimming lessons that Hora gave to Raimond in the nearby dam, as he passed on to the boy his own love of the water. So much of this book gives a sense of the delights and the richness of life, as much as the difficulties and pains of it. Hora emerges as a man who had a strong influence on the course of Raimond's life, and indeed was a father figure to Raimond. His knowledge and intellectual curiosity, his philosophical bent and his stories all had a profound effect on the young Raimond, helping to shape the future course of his life and his interests. The fact that Raimond obviously still remembers so many of these stories testifies to their importance.

It is no surprise that Romulus and Hora became such fast friends. They were both passionate men. They shared an integrity, a moral seriousness, that emerged during their many long conversations. Perhaps the most important lesson that the young Raimond learned from the conversations of these two men was:

> the connection between individuality and character and the connection between these and the possibility of ... seeing another person as being fully and distinctively another perspective on the world. Which is to say that I learnt from them the connection between conversation and Otherness. (pp.72–3)

It's possible to argue that what Raimond learnt here was the beginning of morality – a sense of the uniqueness, and therefore preciousness, of every person. Certainly, his strong moral awareness seems to have sprung from the quest for wisdom and understanding embodied both by his father and by Hora.

Chapter 6 (pp.75–94)

Summary: *Mitru's decline; Christine's illnesses; Mitru's letter to Romulus; Susan, Raimond's half-sister, is born; Mitru's suicide.*

Christine's illness worsens

In this chapter, the narrative shifts between stories of Raimond's life in different places, with his father and with his mother. Gaita begins in the summer of 1954, when he would have been seven or eight, and when he went to Melbourne to visit his mother and Mitru. Their unreliability is underscored by their failure to meet him at Spencer Street station. This stands in stark contrast to Romulus' almost total reliability as a parent; we can see that Romulus has been both mother and father to his son.

An interesting anecdote is included in the narrative at this point. While in the care of the St Kilda police, Raimond took particular pleasure in being allowed to wear the policemen's caps. So much so, that in the future he kept on asking anyone at Spencer Street who was wearing a peaked cap if he could wear it for just a few moments. This may have been 'a small thing' (p.76), but the fact that Raimond kept asking in spite of repeated refusals betokens a remarkable persistence, a strength of purpose and a basic confidence that perhaps were born out of the toughness of his early experiences.

Life for Raimond's mother continued to be wretched, undermined by problems of both physical and mental health. To combat her psychotic illness – schizophrenia? – she was given electric shock treatments. Known as ECT (Electro-Convulsive Therapy), shock treatment is usually administered only to seriously depressed patients. The objective of this treatment is to facilitate recovery by altering the chemistry of the patient's brain. The fact that ECT is usually given only as a last resort indicates the seriousness of Christine's illness. It is also worth remembering that ECT was administered much less humanely in the 1950s than it is today. We can only feel sympathy for Christine in the midst of this plight, all the more so when we learn that the treatment was unavailing.

Raimond recalls that, as he watched his mother suffering from the effects of asthma, he felt 'a pity that was both intense and disturbingly detached' (p.77). The word 'disturbingly' suggests that Raimond, whether at the actual time or at the time of writing, felt guilty about this detachment from his mother's suffering. Why might he have felt detached? Was nature stepping in and kindly protecting him from the worst of his mother's suffering? Or had his long absences from her weakened the natural bond between mother and son? Whatever the truth, we are given a close-up view of a situation that must have brought great suffering to them both.

Mitru's letters to Romulus

At this point (pp.77–81), two of Mitru's letters to Romulus about Mitru's relationship with Christine are interpolated into the story. I find myself wondering how Gaita was able to reproduce these letters here at a distance of so many years. Would it have been possible for him to remember them word for word, or is what is printed in the book a reconstruction from his memory? If so, to what extent is what we read here fiction? Or perhaps Gaita had access to these letters after his father's death and was thus able to reproduce them.

The first letter, which Raimond carried from Mitru to Romulus, contained what Mitru called his 'confession' to Romulus. Its tone is extremely solemn. In it, Mitru revealed that Christine was pregnant and wanted a divorce; that she still respected Romulus 'like no one else' (p.79); that she was very ill with asthma and also mentally ill – 'she has been hearing voices for a few weeks now' (p.79) – and that Romulus had been providing money. The letter also underlines the fact that Mitru greatly respected Romulus and was troubled that his relationship with Christine had undermined their friendship.

Gaita claims to have included these letters 'to convey the quality of [Mitru's] sensibility' (p.77). They show that, despite his very human weaknesses, Mitru was a good man, but certainly not one as worthy of respect as his brother, Hora. Christine, whom Romulus blamed primarily for the affair – he knew her as 'a woman who liked men' (p.83) – appears even less worthy of respect. The letter she wrote to her sister in Germany, implying that Romulus was the father of the child she was carrying and that the family was again intact, was another sign of her chronic inability to accept responsibility for her actions.

It comes as no surprise to learn that Romulus refused Christine's request for a divorce, bearing in mind the moral absolutism he displayed throughout his life. (His later reluctance to allow Raimond to leave the school where he was unhappy simply because he had already started there is an illustration of the same trait.)

The memory that Gaita relates here of his mother's cooking meat for his eleventh birthday is poignant. That he still has a fondness for burnt meat because it reminds him of the rare experience of his mother preparing a meal underscores the extent of his deprivation. Most of us, I imagine, would have taken for granted the maternal care embodied in such a simple act.

Mitru's suicide

With the birth of Susan, Christine's pattern of neglect continued. Gaita paints a picture of deepening domestic dysfunction: Christine, Mitru and the baby living in cramped conditions at the back of a wine saloon; the neglected baby crying with nappy rash; Christine profligately spending money on expensive clothes. Mitru seemed to have suffered the most.

The distress he felt over the neglected baby, the family's financial difficulties, and Christine's repeated infidelities exploded when he hit Romulus following an argument. Worse followed: he attempted suicide by stabbing himself; he sent Hora away after a quarrel, telling him not to come to see him again; he beat Christine with his belt. Finally, he jumped to his death from a nearby tower, the first of a succession of suicides described in this book. Mitru's death was a tragedy. It was a waste of a still young life, with much to offer, and it deprived Hora of a brother and an unborn child of a father. Mitru may have felt that he was 'a wretched man' (p.93) but, as much as anything, it was the circumstances of his life that were wretched.

Vignettes

As well as the overall impression of sadness and waste, many small vignettes stay in our mind from this chapter. There is Gaita's memory of the reconciliation between Christine and Mitru following his attack on her, obviously deeply etched in Gaita's mind, as we can tell from the precision and detail with which he relates it. There is the cruelty of the Catholic priest who refused to bury Mitru because he had committed suicide, a lack of compassion, we imagine, of which Romulus would have been incapable. There is the image of Mitru's body lying in an open coffin, 'his face broken and dark purple with bruising' (p.92) – an image which haunted Raimond for years. And finally, the gloomy epitaph on Mitru's grave – 'Belief in the afterlife is the only hope in us' (p.94) – as if to say that our earthly life contains no such grounds for hope.

Chapter 7 (pp.95–106)

Summary: *Romulus has another motorcycle accident; his skills as a worker; the difference between character and personality; Romulus joins a lonely hearts club and the saga of Lydia begins.*

The chapter begins with an anecdote that shows the power games even young children can play against their parents. Raimond's angry

'You don't love me' to his father after Romulus had smacked him once (p.95), and his later statement that he meant what he said, 'obviously troubled' Romulus (p.96). We are left wondering whether Romulus' distress over his son's words directly led to the serious motorcycle accident of which we soon learn. Given the extent to which Romulus was driven by his emotional reactions, and his statement to Raimond in the hospital, 'Never believe that I don't love you' (p.97), we are inclined to surmise that it did. After all, these were the only words Romulus spoke to his son on the night when Raimond visited him in the hospital. The incident shows us how quickly Romulus' emotional balance could be upset, and also how much Raimond really loved his father; if he had not loved him greatly he would not have felt such a sense of guilt.

Romulus as a worker

Romulus was a remarkably industrious and skilful worker, of astonishing versatility. We can't fail to be impressed by the variety of things he could do or make – not only ironwork, his specialty, but also shoes and clothing, and domestic items such as curtains. He made cigarette holders and knife handles from 'old sheep bones he found in the paddocks' (p.98). This piece of information is somehow emblematic of Romulus' whole life: he was always making something valuable from even the most unpromising materials.

Character and personality – and what it is to be human

Gaita informs us that his father and Hora shared a common belief 'that nothing matters in life as much as to live it decently' (p.101). This belief underpinned their strong emphasis on the importance of character – 'the central moral concept for my father and Hora' (p.101). 'Character', which suggested 'something steady and deep in a person', they contrasted favourably with 'personality', which they believed to be 'superficial and changeable' (p.102). Their common emphasis on the value of that which is lasting and of substance speaks of their moral seriousness and their essential wisdom.

At this point of the chapter, Gaita the philosopher takes over briefly. An interesting aspect of his writing in this memoir is the way he uses his training as a moral philosopher to amplify his discussion of some of the issues raised by his father's life. He briefly interrupts the narrative to reflect on this issue of the distinction between 'character' and 'personality'. In so doing, Gaita addresses one of the central questions of his book: what does it mean to be human? Gaita argues that the sharp division between 'character' and 'personality', common in Baringhup at this time, was limiting in that 'like other sharp divisions, it could not capture the many worthy ways of being human' (p.103). In particular, it worked against his mother. He describes her as being the wrong person in the wrong place at the wrong time. Perhaps, in a more tolerant and broad-minded environment, she may have fared better, but the limitations of the culture in which she found herself 'were partly the reason she could not overcome hers' (p.104).

Gaita recognises and affirms the essential goodness of the people amongst whom he lived at Baringhup, seeing in them 'a distinctively Australian decency' (p.104). At the same time, however, he implies that that decency failed to include an attempt to understand those who, like his mother, were different in some way. To be truly human is to avoid hastily judging those whom we find hard to understand. It is to Gaita's credit that he never judges his mother's behaviour harshly; he recognises how difficult life was for her. Those who condemned her outright failed to see the complexity of her personality, failed to see that she was a person who, as well as having glaring faults, possessed considerable virtues – 'highly intelligent, deeply sensuous' as she was (p.103). In fact, hers was a very human story.

Q Has this book helped you to redefine your sense of what it means to be human?

Lydia

Here begins one of the most dramatic and extraordinary episodes in the book. It is also an episode in which truth seems stranger than fiction.

Why did Romulus become involved with a lonely hearts club? His son cannot answer this question, but without doubt his emotional need at the time must have been very great, and he must have felt very lonely. In this chapter, we are told only the beginnings of the story: Romulus fell in love with Lydia purely by correspondence and as a result became very happy for a time.

Chapter 8 (pp.107–14)

Summary: *Raimond goes to school at St Patrick's College, Ballarat; Christine and Mitru's children are made wards of the state; Raimond tells his mother that he doesn't want to see her; she commits suicide.*

In this chapter, we learn how Christine's troubled life came to an end. Both of her daughters, Susan and Barbara, were made wards of the state after she fell behind with her maintenance payments. She was warned that this would happen 'without compassion or regret' (p.108) – this detail reminding us that the 1950s were, in some ways, harsher than today. It's hard, though, to argue against the matron's verdict that Christine was 'a hopeless case' (p.108), and it is clear that only Romulus' excellence as a father saved Raimond from the fate of his half-sisters.

Most of the material in this chapter is so distressing that it is difficult to read. How upsetting it must have been for Raimond that he 'felt awkward' (p.109) in the presence of his mother, a feeling underscored by the poignant recollection of her dancing to the jukebox in a cafe half-filled with customers. How sad, too, that her rejection by both her husband and her son undoubtedly contributed to her suicide. But we can hardly blame Romulus or Raimond for this. Christine had become such a destructive presence in both their lives that they needed to maintain their distance from her. But this is still a tragic story about a waste of a life.

Gaita feels that Romulus, Hora and probably Mitru all failed to understand 'the degree to which my mother's life and behaviour were affected by her psychological illness' (p.112). Their failure to understand would probably have been shared by most people at the time. Yet, suggests Gaita, there was something in his mother's make-up that perhaps no-one could understand: 'no failing of character, no vice, explains or even describes her incapacity properly to care for her children' (p.112). Her story speaks powerfully of the ultimate incomprehensibility of other people, of the mystery at the heart of some people that even our best efforts cannot penetrate.

That Christine's grave 'remained without a headstone until 1981' shows the 'intense and conflicting emotions' (p.113) that for so long prevented Romulus and Raimond from giving her this simple recognition. But they both must have been thankful that they finally found it in their hearts to do so, with Romulus speaking 'compassionately' of her at the grave (p.114). And although this chapter is profoundly sad, it ends on an elevating note. The last sentence, so elegantly constructed, gives a strong sense of life moving forward in the midst of death. It also speaks of the bonds between humans that create the emotional supports enabling us to hold together in the face of adversity. 'Working together, our sorrow lightened by the presence of a young girl representing new life and hope', writes Gaita, 'we came together as son and husband with the woman whose remains lay beneath us' (p.114).

Chapter 9 (pp.115–40)

Summary: *Both Romulus and Hora offer to adopt Mitru's daughters; Romulus falls into insanity; the bombshell that helped to cause this; Raimond swings into action during his father's illness; the story of John Dunstan.*

The problem of who should care for the orphaned children of Christine and Mitru is the focus of this chapter's opening. Romulus, though seeking to adopt them, failed to maintain contact with the authorities – 'the reason was that he was falling into insanity' (p.117). This sentence, isolated for effect, hits like a sudden blow. And the bombshell that sparked this disaster was the devastating news he learnt about Lydia. After arranging for her to come to Australia with her family and to marry him, Romulus found that 'Lydia was not the woman he imagined her to be' (p.118). What an understatement! That Lydia had failed to tell Romulus that she had long been engaged and was now married must have come as a profound shock – especially for a man who seemed to expect everyone else to behave as honourably as he. 'How could she have done it?' (p.120), he wondered. His deep shock at Lydia's malevolence was the reaction of a man 'with an extraordinary sense of the reality of the ethical' (p.122). Although his life experience had given him the dark view that human beings were 'victims of fate and destined for suffering' (p.122), his mind could by no means come to terms with the reality of a person like Lydia.

Gaita's account of this distressing period in his father's life is coloured by his philosophical bent. In fact, he gives us here real insight into his own sense of life while describing his father's ordeal in the psychiatric hospital. For Raimond, the hospital remained outside the framework of life at Frogmore, which he depicts as a world of sanity, beauty and permanence, a place where 'the hills looked as old as the earth' (p.123). Here he discovered a stability that could not be found in the human world, and as such was very comforting. We are given a sense of how Gaita, as well as older people like Hora, were shaped by this landscape. Gaita writes movingly of its different moods, culminating in the late afternoon light which 'graced the area in a melancholy beauty that could pierce one's soul' (p.124).

Gaita's sense of the tragic

The word 'melancholy' is key here, speaking as it does of Gaita's tragic sense of life which he tells us was nourished by the landscape around him. 'Tragedy', he writes, 'with its calm pity for the affliction it depicts, was the genre that first attracted my passionate allegiance' (p.124). Through the concepts of tragedy, Gaita was able to see Mitru, his mother, his father and Vacek as 'the victims of misfortune, in their different ways broken by it, but never thereby diminished' (p.124). That sense of tragedy must have been both confirmed and heightened by the sight of Romulus in the psychiatric ward, surrounded by greatly disturbed people, anguished at having been given shock treatment.

This section of the chapter is studded with words emphasising Romulus' psychological distress. It hardly comes as a surprise when we learn that he attempted suicide; we could be forgiven for thinking that there must have been a curse on him and the people around him that made them prone to suicide or attempts at it. For Raimond, this time was a turning point; he felt 'changed' (p.125). He knew that he could never again rely on his father's strength to guard him against the sorrows of life.

Raimond must have suffered greatly from the distress of those around him, but he makes light of this. He rarely describes how these traumatic events affected him personally. It would appear that, at the time, he accepted them stoically and got on with his life. But we also need to remember that these events are being recalled at a considerable distance, and so the passage of time may have blunted the emotions he recalls.

John Dunstan

Romulus' incapacity meant that Raimond had to shoulder the responsibility for delivering his ironwork. To help him with this difficult task, he enlisted the help of a friend from school, John Dunstan, whose personal story is interpolated into the narrative. It is another sad story, culminating in yet another suicide. Gaita shows us that John Dunstan was both kind and interesting; his sad and lonely death seems particularly cruel. Perhaps Gaita feels some guilt over his friend's fate, since he gave him advice that turned out to be unwise and may have been a contributing factor in his suicide.

Gaita's sense of comedy

The rest of the chapter includes a number of anecdotes that contain comical elements. The episode in which Vacek appeared suddenly at the window of the house one night and frightened John Dunstan out of his wits is very amusingly told. Gaita has a strong sense of the ridiculous that must have been nurtured by his many experiences of the offbeat behaviour of the people close to him. Then there is the memory of his father's visit to his school with Vacek, both of them looking like tramps.

The scene as it is described is poignant, but it also borders on the ridiculous. I have to admit that I laughed aloud when I read it for the first time; not even the comparison of Romulus with a concentration camp survivor could suppress that response. It is interesting to see how this memory has engraved itself on Gaita's mind: the detail in his description gives it great immediacy. And we can well imagine the 'guilt and shame' (p.136) he must have felt for denying his father.

The most arresting of the three anecdotes is the one which tells of Romulus' sudden announcement that he and Raimond were to go to Sydney in order to shoot Lydia's husband. Romulus made this announcement with the matter-of-factness with which he might have announced his departure on a fishing trip. Planning murder is obviously a serious matter, but the way it is described it also seems absurd and comical, like a scene from an improbable fiction. Interesting, too, is Gaita's recollection of his response to his father's pronouncement; he was not appalled by it, but rather felt convinced 'that sexual love was a passion whose force and nature was mysterious, and that anyone who came under its sway should be prepared to be destroyed by it' (p.137).

The story ends with an unexpected twist, due to Romulus' natural courtesy even when planning a murder as well as Lydia's beauty and her husband's pleasantness gently deflecting his purpose. Yet there still remains the pain of Romulus' thwarted love, a frustration that drove him to madness – a story as old as life itself. And there is Gaita's memory of his father's statement, 'There is no sickness worse than mental sickness' (p.140). With what force those words must have struck the young Raimond: he remembers the exact point where they were on the road when his father spoke them. More than anything, Gaita remembers his father's 'strong, bare, sun-darkened arms on either side of me', arms which he felt protected him from the 'terrible meaning' (p.140) of these words. Even in the midst of his affliction, Romulus remained for his son a powerful presence and defence.

Chapter 10 (pp.141–59)

Summary: *Romulus' superstitions; reversals in Hora's life; Romulus buys a house on the outskirts of Maryborough; Romulus pays fares to Australia for all of Lydia's family.*

We are told more about Romulus' precarious mental and emotional condition in this chapter. Irascible and prone to 'anxious and paranoid outbursts' (p.142), he quarrelled with everyone around him. His instability placed severe strain on his friendship with Hora, the adult to whom he was closest. He also became a prey to superstition, seeing inauspicious signs in the strangest places.

Life for Hora, too, was difficult at this time. Having already lost his brother in tragic circumstances, he was refused by the woman he loved and 'the pain of this loss affected [him] for years' (p.143). This story serves to reinforce Romulus' strong sense of 'our vulnerability to affliction' (p.143). Both Romulus and Hora suffered the further loss of Christine and Mitru's two daughters, who were both put up for adoption. Hora, who was deeply fond of the girls, had to wait thirty years before seeing them again.

Gaita includes a disturbing detail at this point, describing how Susan repeatedly banged her head against the wall or the bedstead at night. Almost certainly, the traumas she must have endured in her earliest years caused this behaviour. The pathology of her parents seems to have been revisited upon her. Considering the trauma that Raimond must have endured as a result of his mother's mental condition, it is a wonder that his own behaviour was not equally disturbed. We might ask how he managed to endure through such a rocky childhood. Perhaps the answer is that he was always convinced of his father's love for him, and even of his mother's, neglectful though she was.

We learn of Romulus' purchase, at his son's instigation, of 'a modest weatherboard house' (p.148) on the outskirts of Maryborough. It's worth remembering that Raimond would have been only sixteen at this time; his ability to convince an adult to make a decision of this magnitude shows that he must have had a maturity well beyond his years. It is clear that the circumstances of his life forced him to adopt adult responsibilities while he was still an adolescent. In a number of different ways, Raimond took responsibility for his father. His clear concern to protect his father's interests shows the deep love he felt for him.

Lydia and her family

Now (pp.149–55) continues the bizarre story of Lydia and her family. Romulus' moral absolutism is evident in his willingness to pay the fares to Australia of Lydia's mother and brother. Despite Lydia's appalling treatment of him, he could not conceive of reneging on a promise. Most reasonable people would have well understood if he had; what is harder to understand is that he didn't.

What follows reads like a soap opera as we learn of the designs which Lydia's mother had on Romulus. She assumed that because Romulus 'was lonely and seeking a wife, he would settle for the mother instead of her daughter' (p.151). The matter-of-fact way in which Gaita reports this outlandish assumption is very amusing, clearly illustrating how his low-key reporting of extraordinary events adds to their impact.

Gaita's quietly comical touch is also evident in the amusing anecdote about the visit of 'M' (whose name is withheld to save him from embarrassment). Again, truth is superior to fiction; the story is so bizarre that it could hardly have been made up. The whole incident must have been distressing to Romulus at the time, not least because he had to ask a guest to leave his house, but it makes very diverting reading. The image of the agitated Romulus ringing a psychiatrist because he had concluded that Lydia's mother had 'gone mad' (p.153) is particularly amusing – even though madness was definitely no laughing matter for him.

Romulus' moral absolutism again

Unhappy at St Patrick's, Raimond defied his father and left to continue his schooling in Melbourne. We see dominant aspects of both their personalities here: Romulus' uncompromising morality in insisting that what one begins one must finish, no matter what; and Raimond's determination and confidence in standing his ground. Most probably, Romulus would have seen in his son's behaviour lack of respect for a parent, but it is hard not to admire the strong sense of self that enabled Raimond to stand up to his father's determination. Raimond's strength of character is also evident from his account of his difficulties at St Patrick's. The dominant ethos of most schools in the early 1960s was authoritarian – this would have been especially so in a conservative Catholic school – and it would have taken real strength for Raimond to assert himself in such an environment.

Chapter 11 (pp.161–79)

Summary: *Romulus meets Milka and marries her; his life becomes happier and more stable; Romulus' fellow Yugoslavs continue to take undue advantage of his generosity; Romulus' spiritual life.*

Romulus' life at last takes a turn for the better. Milka, a young Yugoslav divorcée whom Romulus found to be 'just right' (p.161), was to fill a loneliness that must have been considerable. After the bitter disappointment of his first marriage, Romulus' second marriage must have gone a long way towards erasing the pain of that unhappy period. With Milka, Romulus enjoyed a life of 'relative stability' (p.178). Even though 'the house shook with their battles' (p.163), the result, no doubt, of the clash of two strong personalities, Milka decided to stay with Romulus 'because she recognised him to be a good and unusual man' (p.163).

It is interesting at this point to note the kind of husband Romulus was – and the word 'unusual' is again apposite here. His attitudes seem unusually enlightened for the time. He appears to have made little distinction between 'men's work' and 'women's work'. His respect for Milka's independence, we are told, 'was unusual in husbands of his vintage from their part of Europe' (p.163).

Romulus' religious faith

Romulus had 'prayed to God to give him a good wife if he was deserving of one' (p.161) and we could be persuaded that his prayers were answered. In this chapter, Gaita focuses also on his father's religious and spiritual life. We can surmise that Romulus' 'deep need of prayer' (p.169) arose out of the need of a sensitive and highly emotional man for comfort from the afflictions from which he suffered. He prayed to the God of the Old Testament – 'the God of Abraham, Isaac, Jacob and Job' (p.169). These central figures from key books of the Old Testament were all men to whom God was said to have revealed himself in the midst of their various trials.

Romulus' religious impulses would no doubt also have arisen from his deep sense of the sacredness of all life, his 'love of all things living and their regeneration' (p.179). Therefore, to all things living, compassion was due, and Romulus' 'unusually deep' (p.165) compassion truly reflected the vital heart of Christian philosophy. His faith appears to have been simple, strongly believed, and unencumbered by doctrine. It was a sign of his unimpeachable integrity that he lived out his beliefs so powerfully. He appears to have been one of those rare people who have taken seriously the injunction of Jesus: 'if your neighbour asks for your coat, give him your shirt as well'.

It is a pity that so many of those around Romulus fell so short of the ethical standards he followed. I found myself growing angry while reading of how other people took such undue advantage of his bountiful generosity. The anecdote about the man for whose entire family Romulus paid the airfares to Australia is infuriating. That this man reneged on his promise to pay back the money, and even had the gall to offer Romulus a three-quarters-full bottle of *slivovitz* as a present, brings to mind the saying 'no good deed goes unpunished'. It was a sign of Romulus' remarkable quality as a human being that he never allowed the ingratitude of those he helped to close off his willingness to continue giving.

Although he did not share his father's religious faith, Gaita clearly respected it. Romulus' spirituality, Gaita tells us, remained untainted by the eccentricity of his 'spiritualism'. Gaita distinguishes his father's religion from that of his Yugoslav relatives, about whom he writes amusingly. These people were 'overtaken' by religion and there was an 'epidemic' of conversions to evangelical fundamentalism amongst them (p.167).

Romulus' objection to his relatives' religious beliefs was partly due to the fact that he saw the hypocrisy behind them. To him, their 'desire for wealth and prestige' (p.167) was at odds with the essence of religion. He appears to have possessed a clear-sightedness about these people that arose from deep wisdom. This, no doubt, was deepened by the suffering he endured as a result of his mental illness. Gaita raises the age-old question of whether suffering ennobles the sufferer, concluding that 'there is another and different thought, which is that only suffering makes one wise' (p.172).

Chapter 12 (pp.181–200)

Summary: *Romulus' retirement; his life with his animals; his health declines.*

Gaita feels that his father was 'slightly diminished by his retirement' (p.183). It was probably a pity that he did retire; work had played such a vital role in his life and its absence must have created a big gap. It's possible that retirement closed off a vital avenue of creativity for Romulus.

One compensation was that he had more time to spend with his animals. Gaita relates moving stories about his father's remarkable rapport with them, such as the anecdote about the goat whom Romulus believed to be lonely and so bought a mate for it. The story about the bees that were crushed shows that Romulus' compassion went out to even the smallest of living creatures.

From late in this chapter onwards, Gaita gives us the details of his father's decline. Despite the presence around him of those whom he loved and who loved him, he came to the conclusion that 'I'm good for nothing. Just for the rubbish heap' (p.200).

Chapter 13 (pp.201–8)

Summary: *May 1996 – Romulus' last month.*

Gaita's last words about his father, spoken in the eulogy he gave at Romulus' funeral, were that he was 'a man who would rather suffer evil than do it' (p.207). This seems a fitting epitaph for his life; and it is fitting, too, that Gaita ends by telling of Neil Mikkelsen's undying gratitude to Romulus, for saving his life when he fell from the haystack.

CHARACTERS & RELATIONSHIPS

Romulus: 'a good and unusual man'

Key quotes

'My father was not merely skilled, he was a man of practical genius' (p.4).

'He hated lying and believed that only a rigorous truthfulness could give a person the inner unity necessary for strength of character' (p.48).

'My son is everything to me' (p.64).

'From old sheep bones he found in the paddocks he made cigarette holders and handles for the knives he also made' (p.98).

'[He had] an extraordinary sense of the reality of the ethical ...' (p.122).

'He was a passionate man and his madness was passionate' (p.127).

'[Milka] recognised him to be a good and unusual man' (p.163).

'Compassion went unusually deep in my father' (p.165).

'At the centre of his religious sensibility was the idea of a pure heart responsive to those in need' (p.168).

'Sometimes, to be confronted by him was like being confronted by a Biblical prophet, someone whose fierce purity made him transparent to the reality of the values he professed' (pp.174–5).

'My father had no real sense of how beauty in architecture, artefacts, manners, speech or style of eating, for example, could grace our lives' (p.175).

'He could not understand how anyone could prefer to live in ignorance or illusion about anything that mattered to the meaning of their lives' (p.193).

'He was truly a man who would rather suffer evil than do it' (p.207).

At the heart of this story is Romulus' strong and colourful personality. He was a complex man, a man of many parts. He was a man of outstanding faithfulness, as we can see from the wonderful reliability which he displayed as a father. He gave Raimond obvious support and love at every stage of his life, as well as being a reliable neighbour and friend. Indeed, we gain the strong impression that he treated all those he encountered with equal respect, regardless of their status. This respect for life extended also to animals, all of which Romulus treated with kindness and affection. He even felt sorrow at the sight of injury to bees. He was truly a man of enormous compassion and empathy, qualities that no doubt were deepened by his own experience of affliction.

Romulus' conscientiousness extended to his work. His ironwork was always of the highest quality, as befitted a man who was never satisfied with anything less than excellence. He could turn his hand to any kind of practical task – in his son's words, he was 'a man of practical genius' (p.4). His work provided a focal point for his life and a productive outlet for his energies; retirement was a relatively barren time for him, and it was a pity that he did not keep on working until the end of his life.

There was a tough adaptability about Romulus. He had plenty of steel in his backbone, so to speak. He endured enormous hardships at every stage of his life, especially in Germany where he was occasionally imprisoned and beaten by the Gestapo (p.7). He seems never to have indulged in self-pity. Gaita describes his father as 'spartan'; Romulus spurned luxury, although he obviously enjoyed his *slivovitz* and his cigarettes.

Yet, for all his strength, Romulus was vulnerable to affliction. When Raimond saw him in the psychiatric hospital for the first time, his belief in his father's fortitude was undermined. 'I had absorbed past sorrows against the sure confidence of my father's strength', he writes; 'I knew that, whatever was to come, I could never do so again' (p.125). Romulus' sensitivity enriched his life immeasurably, but it also made him vulnerable to immeasurable suffering. And he did suffer greatly. To illustrate this, we need look no further than his response to Lydia's deceit towards him, or the agonies of anxiety he often felt on behalf of Raimond. Or his melodramatic and alarming statement to Raimond as he drove his motorcycle wildly on the day before his wife's funeral: 'Tomorrow there will be three coffins' (p.111). His view of life was dark and fatalistic. All in all, he lived with great intensity, and while this made his life interesting, it would also have made it difficult, to say the least. His deeply passionate and emotional nature predisposed him to mental illness – 'he was a passionate man and his madness was passionate' (p.127).

For all his goodness as a human being, it cannot have been easy to live with Romulus. His volatility must have contributed mightily to the wild battles between himself and Milka. He was, in many ways, an extremist – not only of extreme emotions, but also of extreme and absolutist moral standards. While his deep moral sense was clearly a virtue, it became a limitation when unsoftened by a capacity for flexibility or compromise. Most of us would consider, for example, that his insistence that Raimond should finish his schooling at St Patrick's simply because he had started it there was unreasonable, because it placed a concern for principle ahead of the need for happiness.

Romulus' rigorous moral standards could be seen in his unswerving integrity. He was honest in his actions and truthful in his words, and he expected other people to behave in the same way. He would tell people quite frankly if he thought they were liars or cheats, yet he never excluded them from his society. In his mind, nothing could erase their inalienable dignity as human beings.

Above all, Romulus was a wonderful father. That Raimond's life turned out successfully despite the trials of his early years is in no small degree due to Romulus. We see a clear case of a good single-parent family being far more beneficial to a child than a bad two-parent family. Despite everything, Raimond always knew he was loved. Romulus fully encouraged his son's intellectual curiosity and hunger for knowledge; he encouraged Raimond's reading and provided many hours of good conversation. He was a great teacher for Raimond; no doubt Romulus' deeply thoughtful and profoundly moral approach to life helped to develop Raimond's special interest in moral philosophy.

Raimond Gaita: author and philosopher

Key quotes

'Inclinations to delinquency ran strong in me ... At a certain point in my teenage years, intellectual interests ran stronger than they did' (p.72).

'... tragedy, with its calm pity for the affliction it depicts, was the genre that first attracted my passionate allegiance: I recognised in it the concepts that had illuminated the events of my childhood' (p.124).

There are two Raimond Gaitas under consideration here: Raimond Gaita the child and adolescent; and Raimond Gaita the author, looking back over his own life and the lives of the people around him. Firstly, then, what impressions do we gain of Gaita the author? My strongest impression is that he is very generous. He is reluctant to judge people, preferring instead to seek to understand them and their motivations. He seems to have acquired from his father the capacity to accept people simply because their humanity itself confers dignity upon them. He never suggests that their weaknesses diminish their inherent value as human beings.

Gaita tells his story without any trace of bitterness or recrimination, so that as readers we are bigger, rather than smaller, for having shared it. He always makes light of the trials he underwent. Perhaps in telling his own story he found a way to come to terms with particular events in the past. In *The Philosopher's Dog* he quotes Isak Dinesen's observation that 'all sorrows can be borne if you put them in a story or tell a story about them'.[6] By telling of our experiences, we can objectify them, bringing them into the open and reducing the negative power they may have over us.

Our impression of Raimond as a child and a teenager is, in vital ways, of a piece with our impression of him as an adult. He survived his childhood, despite everything, with confidence and capability intact. He appears to have just proceeded with his life, no matter what the difficulties. He knew he was loved, even by so neglectful a mother. Out of the fire of his early trials, toughness and persistence were born. Many stories in the book attest to this. Think, for example, of his persistence in asking to wear

6 Gaita, *The Philosopher's Dog*, p.77.

the caps of railway officials or policemen, even after being repeatedly refused. Or again, there was the time when he successfully delivered all of his father's ironwork when Romulus was too ill to do so himself.

One of the leading edges of Gaita's personality, both as child and adult, is his deeply philosophic bent. As a youth, at times he demonstrated 'inclinations to delinquency', but 'at a certain point in my teenage years, intellectual interests ran stronger than they did' (p.72). In these interests, he was greatly encouraged by his father, but especially by Hora. Raimond's philosophical outlook took shape in his early years; the traumatic events of these years strongly darkened his view of life, so that 'tragedy, with its calm pity for the affliction it depicts, was the genre that first attracted my passionate allegiance' (p.124). In this, Raimond was surely his father's son.

Christine: 'a woman who liked men'

Key quotes

'Men found her attractive beyond her physical features because of the way she combined vivacity and intense, haunted sadness' (p.6).

'... she had the arresting presence of someone who experienced the world with a thoughtful intensity' (p.31).

'Desperately lonely, she was glad of any conversation that came her way ...' (p.31).

'I remember her as cheerful and lively, even when she had hallucinations' (pp.83–4).

'I do not know what my father thought, but I know that his demeanour towards her was almost always of someone who saw her more as a helpless cause rather than a free agent of other people's misfortune' (pp.112–13).

The story of Christine Gaita is tragic, as are all stories of wasted lives. If we ask the question: 'Does suffering ennoble a person?' and use Christine as a test case, we would have to answer 'no'. Her emotional pain could only be healed by death – or so she thought. She appears to have been a person within whom the impulses towards life and towards death were at war, and the impulse towards death won out. Gaita poignantly describes her, after her suicide attempt, as looking 'as though she had returned from the dead, unsure about the value of the achievement' (p.32).

It is clear that Christine had many good qualities – indeed, it is hard to imagine a man like Romulus being prepared to marry her in the first place unless he had seen something of great value in her. She was an intelligent and interesting woman, possessing considerable vitality and cheerfulness even when she was ill. Neil Mikkelsen, who looked for the best in people, described her as a 'woman of substance' (p.31).

She was a deeply sensuous woman, physically attractive and powerfully sexual, with equally powerful sexual needs. It might have been easy to dismiss her (as many people did) as an outrageously promiscuous woman, but there was far more to her than her sexuality. She was by no means superficial; Gaita remarks that 'men found her attractive beyond her physical features because of the way she combined vivacity and intense, haunted sadness' (p.6). It isn't hard to imagine how a man like Romulus would find these qualities attractive.

By any standards, Christine was an atrocious mother, unable to care for any of her three children even in the most basic ways. As a wife to Romulus, and then as a partner to Mitru, she was compulsively unfaithful. Her tongue could be vicious and cruel. It is hard to overestimate her degree of responsibility for Mitru's suicide. And yet despite all this, Gaita is reluctant to judge her harshly. She emerges as a person more deserving of pity than contempt, a person in the grip of an emotional illness over which she was powerless. Gaita wisely doesn't try to explain her behaviour; rather, he suggests that there was a mystery about her that, ultimately, no-one could explain.

Nevertheless, we do wonder what could have led her to turn out as she did. We can imagine how difficult it must have been for a woman of her background to settle down in a small country town on the other side of the world. Her need for intellectual stimulation could not be met. She was desperately lonely, craving company and the sense of security it can bring. Perhaps this powerful need was behind her promiscuity, as if in each new liaison she sought the feeling of emotional security she lacked.

Many of her neighbours must have contributed to her unhappiness and loneliness because of the harshness with which they judged her. Many of them made no attempt to conceal their dislike of her, a contempt that Gaita suggests 'was partly the cause of her failings as much as it was a response to them' (p.104).

At one point of the narrative, Gaita writes of 'the division of the human spirit in that part of the world at that time' (pp.102–3) into the two categories of 'character' and 'personality'. His mother, he contends, was a victim of that simplistic categorisation which 'like other sharp divisions ... could not capture the many worthy ways of being human' (p.103).

Hora: a remarkable man

Key quotes

'Hora was particularly handsome. His high forehead, his large eyes and his mouth gave his face an aspect that reminded me in later years of Albert Camus' (p.15).

'Each week he carried groceries, fruit and anything else we needed, in a heavy sack on his back from Moolort to Frogmore' (p.45).

'Hora's stories were always of men with ideals, devoted to science or to humanity ...' (p.71).

'He read, as few people do, with an openness to the possibility of being radically altered' (p.73).

Hora, Romulus' great friend, was an attractive man in every sense of the word. Like Romulus, he was a multifaceted individual: a scholar and philosopher, a keen and strong swimmer, a true mentor to Raimond. Above all, he was a great friend to many, a man of extraordinary kindness. He willingly and capably acted as a substitute father for Raimond when Romulus was ill; he performed many onerous, practical tasks for others; and he offered to adopt his orphaned nieces, even though he had no female help to do so. There's no doubt that Hora was family to the Gaitas; his story shows us that family is who we feel it is, that those who are not technically 'family' can be closer to our hearts than our blood relations.

Hora demonstrated a basic stability that was lacking in his unfortunate brother, Mitru, and also in Romulus. At times he exercised a restraining influence on Romulus when he was in his more intemperate moods, such as when he lost his temper while smacking Raimond. Hora was a great mainstay for Romulus, and Romulus must have missed his presence greatly when he moved to Melbourne.

He seems to have been constitutionally much stronger than Mitru, fortunate to escape the mental and emotional troubles that plagued his brother. When Gaita describes Hora in his role of surrogate father, we are given a powerful sense of the pure happiness that a bond with a strong, stable adult can bring. Particularly memorable is the section in which Gaita describes the happy days in the dam, when Hora taught him to swim and told him his stories. Hora was a great teacher and a great companion.

Gaita recalls that Hora read 'as few people do, with an openness to the possibility of being radically altered' (p.73). The word 'radical', indeed, could well be applied to Hora, as he was a free thinker, reluctant to be forced into any mould. His lifelong aversion to Communism, stemming from his sufferings under this system in Yugoslavia, is hardly surprising; his strong belief in the rights and the integrity of each individual would have been at odds with Communist ideology. He was an idealist and, like Romulus, was reluctant to compromise his beliefs. It is not surprising that his thinking was deeply marked by his readings of the works of Alexander Solzhenitsyn, a dissident who wrote of the oppression of life under Russian Communism.

Like Romulus, Hora was passionate. When Raimond made remarks that Hora considered to be sympathetic to communism, Hora refused to speak to Raimond for over a month. His anticlericalism was 'ferocious', yet he showed deep respect for the essential philosophy of Christianity (p.72).

Mitru: a likeable man

Key quotes

'I became close to Mitru and very fond of him. He was gentle, quick to laughter and with a wit that showed the sharpness and delicacy of his intelligence. I did not then, or ever, fully know the degree of his pain' (p.26).

'My father was very fond of Mitru because he was so evidently a good man, but he did not respect him as much as he did his brother' (p.82).

'It was a measure of my affection for him, and my sense of his desperation, that I did not resent him for beating my mother, even though I saw him do it and even though she complained bitterly to me, showing her many bruises' (p.90).

'In his own eyes Mitru was a wretched man' (p.93).

'I know that he would have been mortified and frightened by his capacity for such violence' (p.93).

'No one knows why Mitru killed himself' (p.92).

Mitru, Hora's younger brother, was another of the tortured spirits we meet in this book, a man pushed past the limit of his endurance. He was obviously a likeable man, of whom Raimond was very fond. Even the fact that Mitru was instrumental in breaking up his parents' marriage was unable to destroy his affection for him.

It is, of course, easy to fault Mitru's behaviour, but again we notice that Gaita himself is, as usual, reluctant to judge him. Mitru's story is a very human one. He was a good man who made bad decisions and was destroyed by their consequences. It is not as if he deliberately set out to cause harm. And it is not as if Mitru was uncritical of himself – rather, he tortured himself over many of his actions and was 'frightened by his capacity for such violence' (p.93). His relationship with Christine was mutually destructive, and his distress was compounded by the spectacle of seeing his own children so flagrantly neglected by her.

Mitru's death was horrible and unnecessary, although obviously he did not see it that way himself. Gaita invites us to sympathise with this man; it is hard to imagine the desperation that led him to commit so totally self-destructive an act as his suicide. Gaita's account of it inspires an almost mystical horror. We are left to contemplate how easily a person's life can go awry.

Vacek: 'a little mad'

Key quotes

'He lived in the hills outside Maldon, between two granite boulders sealed with corrugated iron, branches and bits of timber' (p.65).

'Vacek's sense of communion with animals extended to the smallest creatures ... His feelings for human beings were no less open-hearted' (p.67).

Vacek's inclusion in this story makes for very entertaining reading; reading about the offbeat and the strange is usually entertaining. But all eccentrics are eccentric in their own way, and few readers would have known of anyone quite like Vacek. Demonstrably insane, he lived between two boulders, talked to himself, and cooked horrible concoctions in his own urine. Although his appearance could be frightening, he 'was a gentle man', intelligent and 'well educated for the times' (p.66). He was endearing, as we can tell from the delightful anecdote about the time when Orloff the dog ate his sausages and Vacek gently reproved him (pp.66–7).

We learn much about Romulus from his treatment of Vacek. He never treated Vacek with the slightest trace of condescension; thanks to this, Gaita never thought of Vacek as weird. He was accepted as a person 'fully amongst us, rather than at the margins'.[7] Indeed, Vacek appears to have been treated as a member of the family by Romulus.

Milka: an attractive woman

Key quotes

'She was twenty-nine and, as [Romulus] put it, "just right, not too tall, not too short, not too fat, not too thin, not too dark, not too light". In fact, she was very attractive, in appearance and in personality' (pp.161–2).

'She was always open and affectionate with me, without ever pressing her claims as a stepmother, and was grateful for whatever acknowledgment I accorded her in this regard' (pp.178–9).

After the disasters of his first marriage and of the interlude with Lydia, Romulus finally found a measure of marital happiness and stability with

7 Gaita, talk at Writers' Festival.

Milka. Perhaps there is something in the saying 'third time lucky'. We learn that 'the house shook with their battles' (p.163), but possibly it could not have been otherwise with two such strong personalities. Milka was clearly a steadying influence for Romulus; the latter section of the book contains a number of scenes of settled, happy domestic life.

It was very much to Milka's credit that she refused to be put off by the more difficult aspects of Romulus' personality, particularly the symptoms of his mental illness. She probably sensed that although life with him would not be easy, it would be rewarding.

THEMES, IDEAS & VALUES

Dysfunctional families and childhood trauma

Key quotes

'Childhood as we now know it, a space apart from the adult world, a life of its own, did not exist in that part of the world at that time' (p.2).

'I spent many nights alone at Frogmore. I was six years old and the nearest house was half a kilometre away. Naturally I was frightened' (p.29).

What impact does early childhood trauma have on those who suffer it? Are the effects of such trauma always carried into adult life? These are questions implicitly raised by *Romulus, My Father.* Gaita begins his book with an arresting account of his father's troubled childhood: a violent uncle, a home without a father, his early years spent mostly away from his mother. We may wonder how great an influence such untoward circumstances were in shaping Romulus' later life. On the one hand, it's possible to argue that as a result of such hardships he was toughened up and became a survivor; on the other hand, we can't help feeling that he would have been less predisposed to the emotional distress of his adult life had his childhood circumstances been more stable.

Raimond's early childhood was difficult, too. Above all, his mother's instability and emotional problems cast a shadow over his life until her death – and then, of course, there would have been the distress occasioned by the tragic circumstances of that event. Like his father, Raimond developed a sturdy capacity to battle on through adversity, to adapt, but this must have come at a heavy price. His could not have been the carefree childhood enjoyed by many children of that time. There were periods when he drifted towards juvenile delinquency. And the struggle of his life must have absorbed a great deal of his energy.

Later, Raimond's half-sisters, the children of Christine and Mitru, showed clear signs of suffering from the instability of their early childhood. Their mother could not care for them properly in their most vulnerable years. They were shunted from one set of carers to another; the strain showed in Susan's behaviour of repeatedly banging her head against the bedstead at night (p.145). Once again, we see how children suffer because of the shortcomings and problems of their parents.

If these stories of childhood unhappiness composed the entire picture, Gaita's book would indeed be bleak. But Gaita places alongside them far more inspiring stories. We are told of those positive influences that enable people to overcome the effects of past difficulties. Raimond's mother, for example, is plainly inadequate as a parent, but his father provides a sound role model and source of inspiration for his son. And when Romulus is unable to look after Raimond, Hora takes his place as a remarkable father substitute. The message we are given is that a person's fate need not be irrevocably shaped by early misfortune, provided that healing influences are at hand.

Q To what extent can people recover from unfortunate circumstances in early life?

Depression, mental illness and suicide

Key quotes

'But the occasional conversation with a local farmer or trip to Maldon could not support her in her struggle against her demons' (pp.31–2).

'In his own eyes Mitru was a wretched man' (p.93).

'… my heart broke when I saw my father in the ward before he saw us, in a room full of visibly disturbed people, some obviously insane, and he shrunken and bewildered' (pp.124–5).

'[John Dunstan] came to Melbourne, failed his matriculation, became lost and unstable and, four years later, jumped to his death from the housing commission flats in Carlton' (p.130).

It is difficult to read this book without being constantly reminded of how easily things can go wrong with humans and their minds, and of how readily life can be destroyed. We are reminded not only of the heights to which people can rise, but also of the depths to which they can sink.

At the heart of the human being is this unfathomable mystery of self-destruction. The competing impulses towards life and towards death can be mixed up in the same person, as they are, for example, so clearly in both Romulus and Christine. In Gaita's memoir, we learn of no fewer than three suicides: those of Mitru; Christine; and John Dunstan, Raimond's friend from school. On top of all this, Romulus himself attempted suicide in the midst of his emotional distress.

I found myself wondering what could have predisposed so many people from the same small area to fall into such distress. Was it the strain of adapting to life in a very different and unfamiliar environment on the other side of the world? The trauma of their early life circumstances? A sense of isolation? Perhaps we can never really know. Gaita wisely doesn't attempt to explain these things; he seems to imply that mental illness is too mysterious for us fully to fathom it. Even today, when we pride ourselves on our understanding of ourselves, we still know relatively little about the mind and its workings. How much less would have been understood back in the 1940s, 1950s and 1960s. And how difficult life would have been for the sufferers of mental illness. Today, although most people no longer hold medieval views of mental illness, it is still stigmatised and still a source of embarrassment. We still find it hard to be as open about mental illness as about physical illness.

I was impressed by Gaita's comment about Mitru's death: 'No one knows why Mitru killed himself' (p.92). Wisely, he refuses to settle for simple, one-track answers, implying that human beings are ultimately mysterious. Admirable, too, is Gaita's avoidance of the dreadful moralising in which some people tend to indulge when they discuss suicide. In *The Philosopher's Dog*, he comments approvingly on the attitude of the philosopher Schopenhauer to this problem. Schopenhauer, he writes, 'caught something important in the attitude to suicide of people like my father when he said that the problem of suicide is too deep for morality'.[8] Gaita's viewpoint on this matter would appear to be very similar to his father's. I found the real villain of this book to be the local priest who

8 Gaita, *The Philosopher's Dog*, p.146.

refused to bury Mitru because he had killed himself, an attitude that could hardly be further from that of Romulus.

Q Why does mental illness make people feel so uncomfortable?

Loneliness and its effects

Key quotes

'I spent many nights alone at Frogmore. I was six years old and the nearest house was half a kilometre away. Naturally I was frightened' (p.29).

'Desperately lonely, she was glad of any conversation that came her way ...' (p.31).

'Not long after the camp was dispersed, Vacek began to lose his mind. He lived in the hills outside Maldon, between two granite boulders sealed with corrugated iron, branches and bits of timber' (p.65).

'My father told the story that one evening he prayed to God to give him a good wife if he was deserving of one' (p.161).

All of the central figures in this story suffered from varying degrees of loneliness. As migrants from far away, they had severed their ties with friends and family in their native lands and needed to re-establish those supportive networks in new, unfamiliar surroundings. Furthermore, they found themselves in a remote, isolated area which made that task all the more difficult.

Romulus' marital problems must have added to his loneliness. Until he married Milka in 1964, he lacked a steady and reliable partner to support him. Christine was often sunk in the self-absorption of depression. Soon she abandoned Romulus for Mitru; as a result, Romulus lost both his wife and his friend. It would have been a difficult and lonely task for him to raise a small child in an isolated farmhouse. The story shows us how great Romulus' emotional needs were. Only deep loneliness could have driven him to his involvement with a lonely hearts club. It was probably difficult for him to meet eligible single women in the area where he was living. Lydia's cruel deception plunged him from great hope to deep despair and madness. Like Christine, he too sank into the lonely despair of acute depression.

Yet Romulus managed to find resources to assuage his loneliness. There was his great friend Hora, and as Raimond grew older, he too became a close companion. There were the animals who offered unconditional love. And there was his faith in God, with whom he formed his own relationship through prayer. It is significant that he offered so specific a prayer as the one that he would find a good wife; this must have been his primary need for many years.

Christine, on the other hand, had fewer resources, whether internal or external, to deal with her loneliness. She was an educated, intelligent woman who craved company and good conversation, but these were rarely available. Her desperate need for human affection must have been a factor motivating her promiscuous behaviour. While Romulus was at Cairn Curran, she would have been alone with Raimond, then only a small child. The image of her that stays in my mind is the one of her spending the night beside a log, alone and injured, as if she had given up hope of finding solace in the family home.

Raimond, too, spent much time alone as a child and adolescent, though we wonder if he felt as lonely as his parents. The nights he spent alone in the farmhouse must have been lonely indeed, although at least he had the comfort of the dogs warming his bed. He was an only child, and although he obviously made friends readily with other children he didn't really fit the mould of a 'farm boy'. And yet he had the invaluable resource of his father's company, and also of Hora's, especially welcome when Romulus was unable to care for him. Above all, Raimond came to feel that he had a place in his environment. We see this when he describes the transformative experience of going into the bush to shoot rabbits, but instead discovering a sense that he was at one with everything around him. He had a strong sense of who he was and where he belonged.

Judging by the circumstances of his life, you would think that Vacek must have been very lonely. He lived in the most primitive, isolated housing imaginable. It probably was not coincidental that he began to lose his mind soon after the camp at Cairn Curran was dispersed; this would have removed his human support network. On the face of it,

Vacek's story is bleak, but it does have redeeming features. We learn, for example, of his 'sense of communion with animals [that] extended to the smallest creatures' (p.67). And we also learn that he was fully accepted by Romulus into the Gaitas' home. Romulus always treated Vacek as a friend, without the slightest trace of condescension.

In Mitru, we see a man for whom the loss of his support network proved disastrous. His relationship with Christine was destroyed, as was his friendship with Romulus, a man whom he greatly liked and admired. He fought with his brother, Hora. Above all, and worst of all, he became alienated from a sense of his own value. He came to regard himself as 'a wretched man' (p.93), unfit for the company of others – and so he removed himself from them.

The relationship between humans and animals

Key quotes

'I took the dogs to bed with me and listened to the radio until I fell asleep. Years later I heard someone speak contemptuously of how Aborigines slept with their dogs for comfort and warmth. I remembered how I had done the same, and was amused at the speaker's stupid contempt. I doubt that I would have coped without the dogs' (p.30).

'I asked [my daughter] whether she knew of anyone, or had even read of anyone, who treated animals more kindly than her grandfather. She immediately replied that there was no one' (p.189).

Animals play an important part in this story. They are, in fact, characters in their own right. They provided immense entertainment and comfort for both Romulus and Raimond, and the anecdotes about them provide tremendous entertainment for us as readers.

I found one of Romulus' most attractive characteristics to be his very humane attitude towards animals. It has been said that one of the measures of a person's humanity is the way they treat animals, and Romulus treated them very well indeed. His kindness extended to all living creatures; he showed no trace of the human chauvinism that regards humans as the measure of everything and animals as an inferior species of little innate value. When his favourite animals died, such as Orloff the dog, he grieved for them as one would grieve for another human.

At the same time, Gaita makes a point of explaining that his father always displayed 'a wisely judged sense of the radical difference in kind between human beings and animals, even though he sometimes blurred that distinction in conversation' (p.188). And not just in conversation – who could forget Romulus' practice of taking his dogs to the drive-in movies, 'convinced that they enjoyed them' (p.188)?

Q Write about an animal you have known well.

Q Do you share Romulus' views about the importance of animals?

What does it mean to live well?

Key quotes

'I have never known anyone who lived so passionately, as did these two friends, the belief that nothing matters so much in life as to live it decently' (p.101).

'… he never intentionally caused suffering to anyone' (p.207).

The question 'what does it mean to live well?' is implicit in the text, for we are constantly aware of Romulus' concern to live a moral life, and to maintain the values which he saw as central to that. Raimond Gaita tells us that his father held the view that 'nothing matters so much in life as to live it decently' (p.101). But what did 'to live decently' actually mean to Romulus? Above all, it meant to honour the inalienable dignity of human beings, to recognise that nothing should be allowed to diminish that. Romulus believed that no person was unimportant, that each had his or her story to tell. We can conclude that no-one was unwelcome in his home, not even those who had treated him poorly. Romulus was morally very intense, but never moralistic: that is, he was not at all judgmental.

Romulus considered soundness of character to be vital. He especially valued honesty, not from the 'prudential justification' that honesty pays, but from a sense that it was the responsibility of a decent person to be honest. Probably few of us would have encountered a person of such unimpeachable integrity, a person so free of hypocrisy.

Gaita's account of the lives of Romulus and his friend Hora invites us to pay attention to the way we live, to the values we display to the world. This is not to suggest that his book is didactic. Far from it. Without any fuss or flourish we are shown a life which is in many ways exemplary; Gaita allows his father's actions to speak for themselves. *Romulus, My Father* implicitly affirms the importance of compassion, too. Romulus again provides a model of this. We see that life can be testing and distressing, and that nothing matters more to us when we are in trouble than to be strengthened by the steadying concern of others.

Suffering and its effects

Key quotes

'[He had a] sense of all other human beings as his fellow mortals, victims of fate and destined for suffering' (pp.121–2).

'People argue about whether suffering ennobles. There is another and different thought, which is that only suffering makes one wise' (p.172).

No-one, least of all Raimond Gaita, would suggest that there is virtue in suffering for its own sake. His memoir, after all, sometimes almost overwhelms us with its graphic accounts of the emotional and psychological distress to which people can be subjected. We read, again and again, for example, of how acute depression can injure and even destroy human lives.

The harshness of Romulus' life experience developed in him a somewhat fatalistic view of life, a sense that suffering and pain are inevitable. Some may consider this a dark and pessimistic view, but most would admire the patient and uncomplaining way in which he underwent his trials. He was quite stoical in his attitude, and his stoicism produced a strong capacity for endurance. Romulus' life was periodically blighted by mental anguish; at such times, the dark clouds of depression and madness would descend on him. Yet he was a survivor, and he allowed his dark experience to speak to him. The wisdom he derived from it was a sense of the value of struggling and enduring, as well as of the need for compassion for others in their suffering.

The importance of the life of the mind

Key quotes

'All conversation, which meant all living, occurred in the kitchen' (p.24).

'Hora often told me stories as we sailed' (p.71).

A constant theme throughout the book is the growth of the young Raimond's mind, under the tutelage both of his father and, especially, of Hora. We learn how Raimond's growing interest in matters of intellect and philosophy helped to rescue him from his early inclination towards juvenile delinquency. Throughout his early life, Raimond's mind was fuelled by reading, thought and especially conversation.

To me, one of the most memorable sentences in this book is the one quoted above: 'All conversation, which meant all living, took place in the kitchen'. For Raimond, good conversation *was* life, and it transformed an ordinary domestic setting into a place of delight. He was very fortunate to have such richness in such ready supply. One of the most important points that Gaita is making here is that good conversation, the free exchange of ideas, is central to a civilised life. And it is central, too, to the process of bringing people together in fellowship. We can imagine that life in the Gaita home would have been very different from life in many homes today, where television and other electronic media hold centre stage.

Stories were central to Raimond's early intellectual development, whether told by Hora, by Romulus, or by others. Stories not only opened Raimond's mind to worlds other than his own; they also helped to link the past to the present.

Q What part have stories played in your own life?

Australian attitudes towards migrants – the power of names

Key quotes

'Perhaps for good reason, or perhaps merely as an expression of their prejudice against "New Australians" (as immigrants were called), the authorities responsible for assigning jobs at the camp chose not to utilise the many skills of the foreign workers who were almost invariably given menial manual tasks. They were called "The Balts" by most Australians in the area because so many of them came from the Baltic countries' (p.16).

'Those were the days before multiculturalism – immigrants were tolerated, but seldom accorded the respect they deserved' (p.100).

Although European migration to Australia was officially encouraged in the years following World War II, native-born Anglo-Celtic Australians did not regard migrants from eastern and southern Europe as their equals. The names used to describe these newer immigrants, such as 'New Australians', carry overtones of condescension. A term such as 'the Balts' to describe immigrants from the Baltic countries sounds disparaging, or at least disrespectful. By labelling immigrants in these ways, Anglo-Celtic Australians avoided viewing them as people with their own particular merits. Australia in the 1940s and 1950s was far more insular than it is today; multiculturalism had not yet altered the face of Australian culture, and travel by Australians to other parts of the world was still relatively infrequent. These were the days of attitudes such as those embodied by the 'White Australia' policy, with its hostility to the immigration of Asian or 'coloured' peoples.

The fact that Romulus' Australian-born neighbours called him Jack instead of Romulus is another example of the use of a name implying a lack of full respect. 'It occurred to few of the men and women of central Victoria', writes Gaita, 'that the foreigners in their midst might live their lives and judge their surroundings in the light of standards which were equal and sometimes superior to theirs' (p.100). At the same time, we need to remember that migrants such as Romulus and Hora felt immense gratitude at being able to begin their lives again in a free and democratic country like Australia.

Q Do you see any evidence of xenophobia (hostility towards foreigners) in Australia today? What could be the reason for this?

Q Do you believe that it should be Australian policy to take more or fewer migrants?

QUESTIONS & ANSWERS

This section focuses on your own analytical writing on *Romulus, My Father*, and gives you strategies for producing high quality responses in your coursework and exam essays.

Essay writing – an overview

An essay on a literary work is a formal and serious piece of writing that presents your point of view on the text, usually in response to a given topic. Your 'point of view' in an essay is your interpretation of the meaning of the text's language, structure, characters, situations and events, supported by detailed analysis of textual evidence.

Analyse – don't summarise

In your essays it is important to avoid simply summarising what happens in a text.

- A **summary** is a description or paraphrase (retelling in different words) of the characters and events. For example: 'Macbeth has a horrifying vision of a dagger dripping with blood before he goes to murder King Duncan.'
- An **analysis** is an explanation of the real meaning or significance that lies 'beneath' the text's words (and images, for a film). For example: 'Macbeth's vision of a bloody dagger shows how deeply uneasy he is about the violent act he is contemplating, and conveys his sense that supernatural forces are impelling him to act.'

A limited amount of summary is sometimes necessary to let your reader know which part of the text you wish to discuss. However, always keep this to a minimum and follow it immediately with your analysis of what this part of the text is really telling us.

Plan your essay

Carefully plan your essay so that you have a clear idea of what you are going to say. The plan ensures that your ideas flow logically, that your argument remains consistent and that you stay on the topic. An essay plan should be a list of **brief dot points** – no more than half a page.

Include your central argument or main contention – a concise statement (usually in a single sentence) of your overall response to the topic. See 'Analysing a Sample Topic' for guidelines on how to formulate a main contention.

Write three or four dot points for each paragraph indicating the main idea and evidence/examples from the text. Note that in your essay you will need to *expand* on these points and *analyse* the evidence.

Structure your essay

An essay is a complete, self-contained piece of writing. It has a clear beginning (the introduction), middle (several body paragraphs) and end (the last paragraph or conclusion). It must also have a central argument that runs throughout, linking each paragraph to form a coherent whole.

The introduction establishes your overall response to the topic. It includes your main contention and outlines the main evidence you will refer to in the course of the essay. Write your introduction *after* you have done a plan and *before* you write the rest of the essay.

The body paragraphs argue your case – they present evidence from the text and explain how this evidence supports your argument. Each body paragraph needs:

- a strong **topic sentence** (usually the first sentence) that states the main point being made in the paragraph
- **evidence** from the text, including some brief quotations
- **analysis** of the textual evidence, with explanation of its significance and how it supports your argument
- **links back to the topic** in one or more statements, usually towards the end of the paragraph.

Connect the body paragraphs so that your discussion flows smoothly. Use some linking words and phrases such as 'similarly' and 'on the other hand', though don't start every paragraph like this. Another strategy is to use a significant word from the last sentence of one paragraph in the first sentence of the next.

Use key terms from the topic – or synonyms for them – throughout, so the relevance of your discussion to the topic is always clear.

The conclusion ties everything together and finishes the essay. It includes strong statements that emphasise your central argument and provide a clear response to the topic.

Avoid simply restating the points made earlier in the essay – this will end on a very flat note and imply that you have run out of ideas and vocabulary. The conclusion should be a logical extension of what you have written, not just a repetition or summary of it. Writing an effective conclusion can be a challenge. Try using these tips:

- Start by linking back to the final sentence of the second-last paragraph – this helps your writing to flow, rather than leaping back to your main contention straight away.
- Use synonyms and expressions with equivalent meanings to vary your vocabulary. This allows you to reinforce your line of argument without being repetitive.
- When planning your essay, think of one or two broad statements or observations about the text's wider meaning. These should be related to the topic and your overall argument. Keep them for the conclusion, since they will give you something 'new' to say but still follow logically from your discussion. The introduction will be focused on the topic, but the conclusion can present a wider view of the text.

Essay topics

1 'We admire Romulus for his admirable behaviour, yet we feel he must have been a difficult man.' Discuss.

2 'Raimond Gaita's background as a philosopher gives his book its distinctive appeal.' Do you agree?

3 '*Romulus, My Father* can be read as a study of emotional disturbance.' Discuss, with reference to two or three characters.

4 'The main interest in *Romulus, My Father* is Gaita's account of his own childhood and adolescence.' Discuss.

5 'The strength of Raimond Gaita's book is his ability to take us into an unfamiliar world.' Do you agree?

6 'Raimond Gaita sets out to pay tribute to his father, but he is still clear-sighted about his weaknesses.' Discuss.

7 'Christine Gaita is to be pitied rather than condemned.' Do you agree?

8 'The main interest of *Romulus, My Father* is Gaita's depiction of the life of migrants in small-town Australia.' Discuss.

9 'Romulus saw human beings as "victims of fate and destined for suffering". As a result, the book unduly emphasises the dark side of life.' Do you agree?

10 'In *Romulus, My Father* it is hard to separate the comic from the tragic.' Discuss.

11 '*Romulus, My Father* shows how hard it is for people to get along with each other, despite their deep need for companionship.' Discuss.

12 'Through his portrait of his father, Raimond Gaita shows us what he values in life.' Discuss.

13 '*Romulus, My Father* shows us that people are either ennobled or destroyed by suffering.' To what extent is this true?

14 'Romulus demonstrates a way of living which is a model for all to follow.' Do you agree?

15 '*Romulus, My Father* is about the destruction of childhood.' Do you agree?

16 'External events rather than character determine what happens to a person.' Does *Romulus, My Father* show this to be true?

17 '*Romulus, My Father* shows us that even though life can be difficult, it is well worthwhile.' Do you agree?

18 "Hora often told me stories as we sailed." What does *Romulus, My Father* show us about the importance of stories?

19 '*Romulus, My Father* shows the importance of compassion.' Do you agree?

20 "The house shook with their battles." 'Gaita paints a dark picture of domestic life.' Discuss.

Analysing a sample topic

'*Romulus, My Father* shows us that people are either ennobled or destroyed by suffering.' To what extent is this true?

It should not come as a surprise to learn that students who plan before writing up their essays do better than those who do not. A well-made plan gives you as the writer a sense of direction. Making a plan is also an act of consideration to your reader, as what is written with care is likely to be read with ease. It's very important that behind your essay there is a strong sense of authorial control – a sense, that is, that you as the writer know where you are going and how you'll get there.

- Begin by identifying the key words and phrases from the prompt (the question). Words such as 'either' and 'or', 'ennobled', 'destroyed' and, of course, 'suffering' are obviously central.
- The phrase 'to what extent' in the question invites you to avoid the trap of simply agreeing or disagreeing with the prompt. We are

being invited to take a more searching approach than that. On no account begin with the sentence: 'I agree with this statement about the book' – even if you *do* agree, this is a very clumsy formulation and starts the essay on a bad note.

- Clarify what the question is asking you to discuss by rephrasing it in your own words. For example: are the effects of suffering on people in *Romulus, My Father* always either very positive or very negative?
- Brainstorm the topic by gathering together ideas around the key ideas of the question. For example: the either/or dichotomy. Do we have to think in such absolute categories? The word 'destroyed' makes us think of Christine and Mitru, but what about Romulus? He may not have been 'destroyed', but he was certainly afflicted grievously by suffering. On the other hand, it could be argued that he grew in wisdom and compassion as a result of the trials he went through.
- See what we're doing in the dot point above: using words and phrases that are similar in meaning to the ones in the prompt. This keeps us on track – it also varies our use of vocabulary.
- Another hint for staying on track: in every paragraph, have one sentence that directly relates to the question.
- Practise gathering together evidence from texts to support the key points of essay questions. One strategy: create a series of headings and marshal evidence to support each one.
- Use linking words and phrases to connect your paragraphs to each other.
- Beware of 'one-track' responses. Try to recognise complexities: the better answers always do.

SAMPLE ANSWER

"Never believe that I don't love you."
'It is the love between father and son that sustains them both throughout their lives.' Do you agree?

The love between Romulus and Raimond remains tacit throughout much of their relationship. Their attachment is expressed more often through actions than words; feelings tend to crystallise in expressions only when remorse is most deeply felt. While conditions for postwar migrants may have denied them luxury and affluence, the strength of largely unspoken feelings was able to transcend material existence.

Even as the young family struggles in Europe, Romulus displays a fatherly affection that extends beyond most people's conception of such love. Before finding work, Romulus sometimes walks eighty kilometres to obtain milk, beans or potatoes, denying himself so that Raimond can have more. Left exhausted by such efforts to get food, Romulus 'fainted from hunger on more than one occasion'. In Germany, Christina already shows signs of her mental illness, neglecting her baby and leaving it in the care of her family. While this behaviour distances Christina from Raimond, it leads to Romulus having to care for and feed his young son, quickly drawing them closer.

With Christina continuing to oscillate between devotion and malaise after the family emigrates, father and son live a tough and austere existence in rural Victoria. Although a persistent mental presence in their respective lives, father and son spend little time in each other's company. At their most physically distant Raimond travels to boarding school, while his father works multiple shifts in town. The gritty nature of this life enforces a kind of pragmatism that leaves little room for expressions of sentiment or tenderness. After being smacked by his father, Raimond cynically exploits the situation, shouting to Romulus, 'you don't love me'. Involved in a motorbike accident just a few days after, the deeply disturbing effect of this childish utterance on Romulus is made clear to

Raimond: unable to speak properly, the only words that Romulus can wheeze out to his son as he lies in bed are 'never believe that I don't love you'. Having confronted mortality in his accident, Romulus forces out these scarcely uttered words with a determination and urgency that strengthens the bond between them.

Nevertheless, some years later, Romulus and Raimond clash again – this time over what Raimond perceives to be his father's blindness to a disjunction between ideal and real-world ethics. The regularity of these clashes is a major component of their relationship during his teenage years, for Romulus' 'character and illness' and Raimond's youth 'occasionally combined explosively'. It is in one of the more violent explosions that the bond between father and son is brought into sharp clarity for Raimond. After a physical scuffle, Romulus suggests that if they cannot agree, they should not see each other again. Paradoxically, the power of such a break between the two – even in suggestion – compels an even deeper sense of the respect they share: 'I loved him too deeply and knew that after what we had shared at Frogmore, no quarrel could estrange us', Raimond realises.

Like the metalwork so beautifully and precisely wrought by Romulus, the love between father and son is moulded to its shape through care. Once set, however, their attachment is unbreakable. Finding expression for that concern through material and practical means, they do not stoop to the exchange of mere consumer goods as more affluent families do but, rather, value the principles of deep love and respect for each other. Gaita conveys to us the sense that only insecure and needy love finds its way to daily utterances that wait eagerly for reciprocity. In contrast, the kind of love between father and son that sustains them both throughout their lives, Gaita suggests, is expressed through selfless daily actions.

REFERENCES & READING

Text

Gaita, Raimond 2002, *Romulus, My Father*, Text Publishing, Melbourne. First published in 1998.

Further reading

Gaita, Raimond 2011, *After Romulus*, Text Publishing, Melbourne.

——2002, *The Philosopher's Dog*, Text Publishing, Melbourne.

Film

Romulus, My Father 2007, directed by Richard Roxburgh. Starring Eric Bana and Kodi Smit-McPhee.